US CONSTITUTION 101

FROM THE **BILL OF RIGHTS** TO THE **JUDICIAL BRANCH, EVERYTHING YOU NEED TO KNOW** ABOUT THE **CONSTITUTION OF THE UNITED STATES**

TOM RICHEY

with PETER PACCONE

ADAMS MEDIA

NEW YORK   LONDON   TORONTO   SYDNEY   NEW DELHI

Dedication

To our departed fathers, who set this book in motion
decades ago when they shared their admiration for
the Constitution with us as children.

Adams Media
An Imprint of Simon & Schuster, LLC
100 Technology Center Drive
Stoughton, Massachusetts 02072

First Adams Media hardcover edition
September 2024

ADAMS MEDIA and colophon are registered
trademarks of Simon & Schuster, LLC.

Simon & Schuster: Celebrating 100 Years
of Publishing in 2024

For information about special discounts
for bulk purchases, please contact
Simon & Schuster Special Sales at
1-866-506-1949 or
business@simonandschuster.com.

The Simon & Schuster Speakers Bureau
can bring authors to your live event. For
more information or to book an event,
contact the Simon & Schuster Speakers
Bureau at 1-866-248-3049 or visit our
website at www.simonspeakers.com.

Manufactured in the United States of America

1 2024

Library of Congress Cataloging-in-
Publication Data
Names: Richey, Tom (Adams 101 series),
author. | Paccone, Peter, author.
Title: US Constitution 101 / Tom Richey
with Peter Paccone.
Other titles: United States Constitution
one-zero-one
Description: First Adams Media hardcover
edition. | Stoughton, Massachusetts:
Adams Media, [2024] | Series: Adams 101
series | Includes index.
Identifiers: LCCN 2024019293 |
ISBN 9781507223017 (hc) | ISBN
9781507223024 (ebook)
Subjects: LCSH: Constitutional law--United
States. | Constitutions--United States.
| United States. Constitution. 1st-10th
Amendments. | Justice, Administration
of--United States.
Classification: LCC KF4550 .R525 2024 |
DDC 342.7302--dc23/eng/20240610
LC record available at https://lccn.loc
.gov/2024019293

ISBN 978-1-5072-2301-7
ISBN 978-1-5072-2302-4 (ebook)

CONTENTS

CHAPTER 3: THE LEGISLATIVE BRANCH 124

INTRODUCTION

Have you ever been curious about how a piece of legislature drafted over two centuries ago remains the law of the land? Are you wondering what makes the US Constitution so long-lasting (the oldest in the world)? Or do you ever think about how the Constitution impacts your life—from paying taxes to boarding a flight?

If so, *US Constitution 101* is for you. Here you'll learn, in clear, simple language, how this document that impacts every aspect of government was formed, how it operates, and how it impacts you. You'll find entries that cover many topics, such as:

- Which Founding Fathers played significant roles in creating the Constitution
- Why the Supreme Court has the final word on what is constitutional
- How the US Senate is different from the House of Representatives
- Why teachers work for state governments rather than the federal government
- Why the US Post Office has a monopoly on delivering mail
- And more

In a democratic union, each member must understand their governing laws and history in order to understand their rights as citizens. That said, despite the Constitution's impact and popularity, most US citizens know very little about it.

According to a recent study by the Annenberg Public Policy Center, most Americans can only name freedom of speech as a right protected by the First Amendment (there are four others), and a third of Americans can't name all three branches of government.

Fortunately, *US Constitution 101* will give you a thorough understanding of the Constitution, no matter how much you may or may not already know about it. This book first looks into the historical document's story and philosophy (including the events of the Constitutional Convention and how the Constitution was approved). You'll then get an explanation of how the Constitution protects the rights of Americans through its creation and maintenance of the three branches of the federal government—this includes how the federal government and state governments interact with each other. So, let's begin our journey through the most important governing document in the American political system—a journey that begins with "We the People."

Chapter 1

The Creation of the Constitution

To understand the Constitution, it's important to first understand its story. The origins of the Constitution can be traced back thousands of years ago when groups of human beings agreed to live under a set of laws. The political systems of the classical civilizations of ancient Greece and Rome provided the modern world with models of popular government. The influence of the Enlightenment and the American Revolution can be seen throughout the Constitution's articles, sections, and clauses.

Although Americans today generally think quite highly of the Constitution, it was never meant to be an ideal plan of government. It is the product of many compromises and controversies. The following chapter details the compromises and controversies that created the Constitution and provides a basic introduction to the principles of American constitutional government, the Constitution's structure, and methods for interpreting its meaning.

WHAT IS A CONSTITUTION?

Organizing and Limiting the Government

For over 230 years, the Constitution has provided a legal framework for the United States. The Constitution organizes a government that is limited in power and protects the rights of "We the People" of this country. Although the US Constitution is among the most famous and enduring governing documents in the world, it was not the first constitution ever created. The framers of the US Constitution knew of others who, over many centuries, constructed governments that were organized, limited in power, and protective of fundamental rights.

THE RULE OF LAW

John Adams once wrote that the idea of good government was based on "a government of laws and not of men." This idea is summed up in the principle of the rule of law. When the rule of law prevails, the laws are posted and known to everyone, they are fairly enforced, and the people generally follow them. A society has a constitution when a system of laws is established and supported by institutions for making, enforcing, and judging the laws.

No one knows exactly when human beings first attempted to live under written laws, but the earliest-recorded written law was handed down by Hammurabi, a Babylonian king who ruled in Mesopotamia nearly four thousand years ago. Hammurabi's Code is best remembered for its harsh punishments, with most crimes being punished by death or dismemberment. While Hammurabi played a role in establishing the rule of law, his code was handed down from above; the people had no part in their own governance.

GOVERNMENT BY THE PEOPLE

The ancient Greeks demonstrated one of the earliest examples of people administering their own government and making their own laws. After several unsuccessful experiments with different forms of government, the people of the city-state of Athens established a form of government they called *demokratia*, which means "rule by the people." Rather than seeing themselves as subjects who were ruled by a monarch, freeborn Athenian men considered themselves citizens who had a right to participate in their government. Citizens rotated through offices, with some being elected and others being appointed by lottery. Laws were made by popular assemblies, and lawbreakers were convicted by juries of their peers.

POPULAR SOVEREIGNTY

Popular sovereignty is the idea that the people are the ultimate power behind the government, and the laws are made and administered on their behalf. This is distinct from monarchies and dictatorships, in which the ruler holds sovereign power over the people, which the ruler may choose to share (in part) with them at the ruler's discretion.

Although the Athenians were innovative in establishing a government of the people, their system of democracy did little to protect the rights of individuals. In a pure democracy, the majority rules, and there are no rights held by minorities or individuals at odds with the majority. For example, Athenians periodically held votes to "ostracize" citizens, a process that involved nothing more than over six thousand citizens gathering and each writing a name on a shard of pottery. The person whose name was written on the most shards was exiled from the city for ten years, with no reason required and no way for the ostracized citizen to make an appeal. In a more extreme case, an Athenian jury convicted Socrates—one of the preeminent philosophers of classical antiquity—for "corrupting the youth" and denying the gods of the state. Socrates was condemned to death for being a public nuisance, something that today would fall under the constitutional protections of free expression found in the First Amendment.

The Tyranny of the Majority

Typically, when Americans think of tyranny, they imagine an oppressive government ruled by a single corrupt individual, known as a tyrant. However, nineteenth-century political writers, such as Alexis de Tocqueville and John Stuart Mill, pointed out that majorities are equally prone to violating the rights of individuals and minorities when there are no constitutional restrictions on their power.

LIMITING THE GOVERNMENT

Constitutional governments place legal limits on the power of government and government officials, as opposed to absolutist and totalitarian governments, which place no limits on a government's authority. The most valuable thing about the US Constitution is that it places limits on the government's power. The Constitution forms a contract between "We the People" and elected governing authorities, distinguishing between the powers held by the government and the rights held by the people. One of the most important parts of the US Constitution is the Bill of Rights, which spells out specific rights of the people, such as free speech, protection from unreasonable searches, and a trial by jury. The idea of a bill of rights was nothing new to the Founding Fathers; they drew the idea from England's rich constitutional history.

Over five hundred years before the Constitutional Convention, King John (yes, the corrupt king from the Robin Hood legend) was engaged in a civil war with his barons. These barons were nobles who governed regions of King John's England in a decentralized system of government known as feudalism. John had provoked the barons (nobles) and church leaders by taxing via royal decree instead of asking for consent to raise taxes beforehand. Then, in 1215, John met the barons and church leaders at Runnymede, where he signed the Magna Carta (Latin for "Great Charter"), in which he promised not to raise taxes without gaining the consent of an assembly of barons. The Magna Carta set limits on the monarch's power in England, leading to a standing parliament with the authority to make laws. In 1689, William III and Mary II signed the English Bill of Rights, which cemented Parliament's status as a standing lawmaking body and enumerated several rights of the people, including the right to petition and protection from excessive fines and bails.

Although the English have never formally adopted a written constitution, they provided a foundation for the US Constitution by passing a body of laws that limit the powers of government officials and protect the rights of the people.

A FEDERAL REPUBLIC

The States and the People

The United States was founded as a federal republic. A federal system of government divides sovereign powers between a shared federal government and separate state governments. In a republican form of government, the people are considered to be the sovereign authority, though they exercise that authority indirectly through elected representatives. The framers of the Constitution used both federalism and republicanism to create a limited government that would be responsive to the people.

OUT OF MANY

The story of the United States is preceded by the separate stories of thirteen British colonies, which were founded along the Atlantic Coast of North America during the seventeenth and eighteenth centuries. The first of these colonies, Virginia, was named after the "Virgin Queen" Elizabeth I. The first settlement in Virginia was named Jamestown after Elizabeth's successor, James I. Colonists flocked to Virginia in the hopes of expanding their fortunes by cultivating tobacco as a cash crop. Only a few years later, the *Mayflower* arrived in Massachusetts, carrying settlers who were fleeing from religious persecution in England. Prior to the French and Indian War (1754–1763), the tobacco farmers in Virginia and the shipbuilders in Massachusetts had very little direct contact with each other, as each of the thirteen colonies governed itself according to separate charters granted by the monarch. The French and Indian War and its aftermath provided the first major opportunities for cooperation among the colonies.

During the war, Benjamin Franklin published a political cartoon depicting a snake cut up into several pieces, with each piece symbolizing one of the colonies. Below the snake, Franklin gave his fellow colonists a dire warning: "Join, or Die." The colonists did not heed Franklin's warnings during the war, but they did cooperate after the British Parliament announced several new taxes (including the Stamp Act) that would be placed on the colonies to help pay for the war. Colonists from Massachusetts to the Carolinas united to protest against "taxation without representation," believing that Parliament had deprived them of their rights to consent to taxation through their own colonial legislatures. The British then responded by sending additional troops to the colonies, resulting in clashes between colonists and troops that eventually led to the Revolutionary War. In 1776, members of the Continental Congress signed the Declaration of Independence, severing the ties between the colonies and the British monarchy.

One distinctive feature of the Declaration of Independence is that its language did not claim to unify the states in anything other than their independence. The Declaration refers more than once to the newly created states as "free and independent states," not a nation. Although these states cooperated to win independence from Britain, the cooperation ended there for the time being. In 1782, the Confederation Congress adopted a Great Seal that included the Latin motto *E pluribus unum* ("Out of many, one"). The earliest American identities of the Revolutionary era were conscious of the separateness of the states much more than the unity of the nation, and this would have a great impact on the formation of the US Constitution.

A REPUBLICAN FORM
OF GOVERNMENT

In addition to adopting federalism, the Declaration of Independence rejected monarchy in favor of a republican form of government. After declaring that "all men are created equal" and possess inalienable natural rights as a divine birthright, Thomas Jefferson unleashed a long list of grievances that took King George III to task as a tyrannical ruler. Forgotten were the conflicts between the colonists and Parliament that led to the war. The signers of the Declaration of Independence addressed their collective anger toward the king himself.

Common Sense

The strong anti-monarchical tone of the Declaration of Independence can be credited partly to the success of Thomas Paine's popular pamphlet *Common Sense*, published in early 1776. Paine wrote: "Monarchy and succession have laid (not this or that kingdom only) but the world in blood and ashes. 'Tis a form of government which the word of God bears testimony against, and blood will attend it."

Republics are inspired by the ancient Romans, who overthrew their king and replaced the monarchy with a government they called *res publica* ("the commonwealth"). The Roman government was designed to rule on behalf of its citizens, who came together annually to elect government officials. These elected officials held limited power for fixed terms of office. Rather than issue proclamations in the name of a monarch, the Roman government's proclamations were made in the name of "the Senate and the People of Rome." A republican form of government is characterized by the absence of a monarch, and the government is administered on behalf of the people by elected representatives.

The early days of the Roman republic provided an exemplary example of the relationship between the government and the governed. Instead of a hereditary king, the Romans elected two consuls each year who shared executive power and command of the military. Publius Valerius was one of the first consuls to be elected. After Valerius's colleague was killed in battle, people suspected that he intended to be king. At the time, Valerius had been building his house on a hill; many believed he intended the house to be his royal palace. When Valerius heard the rumors, he ordered his house to be torn down in front of everyone and made it a capital offense for anyone to declare themselves king. The people were so pleased with Valerius that they gave him an honorary title, *Publicola*, meaning "the people's friend." Valerius's display of statesmanship demonstrated that the people rule in a republic.

It took many amendments over several decades before the Constitution realized the Declaration's promise of a democratic government in which "all men are created equal." However, from the very beginning, the Constitution declared that the people are the power behind the government, and the division of sovereign powers between the federal government and the states is necessary for citizens to remain in control of their government.

THE ARTICLES OF CONFEDERATION

America's First Constitution

After declaring independence, the Second Continental Congress began preparing a constitution that would create a federal government for the newly independent states. The Congress wanted to create a government that could carry on the war with Britain and establish diplomatic relations with foreign governments, while also keeping its powers limited to avoid pushback from the state governments (who weren't interested in yet another outside government). It took over a year of debate before Congress finally passed the Articles of Confederation in December of 1777. It was not until 1781 that all of the thirteen original states ratified the Articles, finally giving Congress official status as a governing body.

A FIRM LEAGUE OF FRIENDSHIP

The Articles of Confederation declared that the states were entering into a "firm league of friendship" but also stressed that the federal government would emphasize the *pluribus* ("many") much more than the *unum* ("one"). The Articles disclaim the idea of complete unity early on: "Each state retains its sovereignty, freedom and independence, and every Power, Jurisdiction and right, which is not by this confederation expressly delegated to the United States, in Congress assembled." The leaders of the state governments still remembered the tyranny of British rule, and they did not want to leave any room for interpretation regarding the limits of Congress's powers. The states were especially hesitant to surrender any economic powers, such as control of taxation and trade, which remained in the hands of the state governments under the Articles.

The Articles of Confederation established a simple government structure with powers that resembled a permanent military alliance rather than an actual government. The Articles vested federal authority in a unicameral (one-house) Congress, with no independent executive branch or federal judiciary. Nearly all of the powers delegated to Congress related to matters of foreign policy, such as maintaining an army and navy, sending and receiving ambassadors, declaring war, and making treaties. Congress had very limited powers within the United States, such as establishing a post office and a system of weights and measures. While Congress could assess taxes, only the states had the power to collect them.

In order to further protect the security of the states, the Articles could not be amended except by the unanimous consent of every state. While this provision protected the states from having to involuntarily submit to constitutional changes without their agreement, it froze the Articles of Confederation entirely. Any defects would become permanent because it is nearly impossible to get thirteen separate political entities to unanimously agree to any changes.

Federations and Confederations

Both federations and confederations are federal systems of government, with divisions of power between a central government and state governments. However, in a federal system, member states are closely aligned, with the federal and state governments sharing sovereignty. A confederation implies that the member states will largely deal with their own internal concerns, sharing a central government that manages foreign relations.

SUCCESSES OF THE ARTICLES

The Articles of Confederation could boast a few key successes. First, the United States successfully concluded a treaty of alliance with France and won independence from Britain. The Confederation Congress also passed the Northwest Ordinance of 1787, in which all of the states relinquished their land claims north and west of the Ohio River (the present-day Midwest) and agreed that these lands, once settled, would eventually become states. The Northwest Ordinance also closed these lands to slavery, representing the first time that Congress limited the expansion of slavery. This landmark legislation proved that cooperation in order to promote the expansion and general welfare of the United States was possible.

Although the Articles boasted some successes, the powers delegated to Congress were insufficient to help the United States recover economically from the Revolutionary War. There was no system for regulating foreign trade (or even trade between the states), nor was there a federal court system to resolve disputes between the states in an orderly manner. These problems all came to a head in 1786 when a Revolutionary War veteran led an armed rebellion against the government of Massachusetts.

A LITTLE REBELLION

The Failure of the Articles

After the Founding Fathers signed the Declaration of Independence, they needed to finance their ongoing war for independence against Britain. In the eighteenth century, money was largely circulated in the form of coins minted from gold and silver. Because of a lack of silver and gold in North America, banks often distributed paper banknotes that could be exchanged for gold or silver coins. Their value, however, depended on whether they could be exchanged. During the Revolutionary War, Congress issued "Continentals," a form of paper currency that could theoretically be exchanged for gold and silver at a later date. However, the continual printing of Continental notes completely tanked the value of this paper currency. Americans began saying that something was "not worth a Continental" to indicate that it was completely worthless.

Although the Articles of Confederation provided a framework for state governments to cooperate to win their independence, the aftermath of the war left most states' economies in shambles. Since the Articles contained no mechanism to govern trade with foreign nations (or between the states), thirteen separate economies existed alongside each other. Congress and the individual states themselves had plunged the US government into debt to pay for the war. Massachusetts, the cradle of the Revolution, struggled to recover as the state government tried to manage its debts while Revolutionary War veterans returned home without the pay they had been promised.

SHAYS' REBELLION

One of these unpaid veterans was Daniel Shays, who had attained the rank of captain after five years of service in the Continental Army. Like many other veterans, Shays found himself in financial trouble, unable to pay his debts without the promised pay. While those in Shays' situation hoped for debt relief from the state governments, Bostonian merchants had their own problems, as their European trading partners insisted on being paid with gold or silver after the war ended. As a result, no debt relief came to the Massachusetts farmers, and state authorities began foreclosing on farmers who had fallen behind on their mortgage payments. Understanding foreclosure to be a legal process, Massachusetts farmers sought to save their livelihoods by taking up arms and forcibly closing courthouses during the summer of 1786.

By early 1787, the improvised rebellion had grown into a force of four thousand men led by Shays and other former Continental Army officers. The group's goal had progressed from closing courthouses to overthrowing the Massachusetts state government. After almost half a year of open rebellion, Shays' Rebellion was finally stopped with the help of private funds from prominent Boston merchants.

Shays' Rebellion exposed key weaknesses in the Articles of Confederation. While the Articles gave Congress authority over war and peace with foreign nations, Congress had no authority to assist states in responding to insurrectionary violence. Even if the Articles had granted this authority to Congress, the funds were not available because Congress couldn't collect taxes from the states. "No money is paid into the public treasury," James Madison lamented, "Not a single state complies with the requisitions." Madison's warning reflected a growing feeling from elites that the Articles did not give the central government enough power to ensure peace in the newly formed country.

Jefferson's Perspective

While George Washington and James Madison panicked over the rebellion in Massachusetts, Thomas Jefferson presented a different perspective from distant France. "I hold it that a little rebellion now and then is a good thing," he wrote to his lifelong friend Madison, "and is as necessary in the political world as storms in the physical."

THE ANNAPOLIS CONVENTION

As Shays' Rebellion was heating up in Massachusetts, a convention took place in Annapolis to address the problem of trade between the states. Several states had placed tariffs (taxes on imports) on goods from other states. These taxes impaired economic growth by discouraging commerce between the states. Organizers hoped that every state would be represented, but only five states sent representatives. Although the delegates talked of improving trade between the states, they knew progress would only happen if more states got involved. Attendees at Annapolis included James Madison of Virginia and Alexander Hamilton of New York, who both envisioned organizing a larger convention in Philadelphia the following year.

THE CONSTITUTIONAL CONVENTION

Starting from Scratch in Philadelphia

By early 1787, many members of Congress knew that the Articles of Confederation weren't providing a stable government or economic prosperity in the United States. However, there were disagreements about whether the Articles should be replaced or merely amended. Congress called for a convention to meet in Philadelphia in May, but limited its mandate by declaring it to be "for the sole and express purpose of revising the Articles of Confederation." James Madison, however, had recently received books from Thomas Jefferson on subjects ranging from history to economics to political science. Madison used ideas from these books to construct an entirely new plan of government to present at the upcoming convention.

THE GREAT COMPROMISE

When the Constitutional Convention convened in Philadelphia, one of the first matters to be discussed was James Madison's plan for a new constitution, known as the Virginia Plan. The smaller states, who had equal votes in Congress under the Articles, were not very receptive to the Virginia Plan's proposal for a bicameral (two-house) Congress. In this plan, states would be represented in both houses based on their populations. At the time, Virginia was the largest state, with a population greater than that of the five smallest states combined. The New Jersey delegation countered Virginia's large-state plan with a proposal to retain the unicameral (one-house) Congress from the Articles, with each state continuing to cast one vote. The convention appeared to be at a standstill, as small states wanted to retain representation and larger states were seeking more of it.

The standoff between the large and small states was broken by a compromise from Connecticut—a state with a middling population—known as the "Great Compromise." The Connecticut proposal featured a bicameral legislature that included a "lower house" (the House of Representatives) where the states would be represented by population, and an "upper house" (the Senate) where each state would be represented equally by two senators. The convention delegates accepted Connecticut's proposal because it balanced the interests of large and small states.

THE THREE-FIFTHS COMPROMISE

Although the dispute between the small and large states over representation in Congress had been resolved, there remained a conflict between the slave and free states over how to count enslaved people for representation in the House of Representatives. Delegates from the Northern states (which had few enslaved people and were in the process of passing gradual emancipation laws) argued that enslaved people should not be counted at all since the slave states did not give enslaved people any political rights. However, since enslaved people made up between 30 and 40 percent of the population in many Southern states, Southern delegates insisted that they be counted.

Again, a compromise was reached. The so-called Three-Fifths Compromise was an agreement to count each enslaved person as three-fifths of a person for the purpose of determining representation in the House of Representatives. In return, a clause was inserted into the Constitution that would allow Congress to ban the international slave trade twenty years after the Constitution took effect (which it did in 1808). This compromise was partly founded on the presumption that the enslaved population would eventually decline. Although it is impossible to reconcile the Three-Fifths Compromise with any idea of justice, it allowed for the Constitutional Convention to continue its business of constructing a governing document that all of the states (large, small, slave, and free) could accept.

Hamilton's Plan

Alexander Hamilton, a delegate from New York, believed that the convention did not go far enough in establishing a strong central government. His plan featured a governor who held executive power, who would serve for life (unless removed from office), and who would have the power to appoint state governors. After Hamilton presented his plan, the convention adjourned for the day. It was never again discussed.

STRUCTURE AND POWERS OF THE GOVERNMENT

The convention delegates adopted Madison's initial proposal for the federal government to be split into three branches. The executive power would be placed in the hands of a president of the United States, who would operate independently from Congress to administer the government and enforce the laws. This president would be elected by an Electoral College, in which each state would be represented according to its total number of senators and representatives (giving the large states more electors and the small states a larger number relative to their populations). The framers also agreed to create a judicial branch with a Supreme Court at its head.

THE SIGNING OF THE CONSTITUTION

Although thirty-nine delegates to the Constitutional Convention signed the finalized document on September 17 (a date formally commemorated as Constitution Day since 2004), there was one problem: The delegates had no authority other than to recommend amendments to the Articles to Congress. The proposed Constitution would not become official until conventions in at least nine of the thirteen state governments ratified it. Some of the states did not want to give up the expansive sovereign authority they enjoyed under the Articles of Confederation.

Additionally, not every delegate to the Constitutional Convention signed the document. When the members of the New York delegation (except Hamilton) realized that the convention was exceeding its mandate to amend the Articles, they went home to report back to their governor. Elbridge Gerry of Massachusetts and George Mason and Edmund Randolph of Virginia stayed through the entire convention but refused to sign the document, foreshadowing the spirited debates that were to come over the Constitution's ratification.

THE RATIFICATION DEBATE

Federalists versus Antifederalists

Before the Constitution could have the legitimate force of law behind it, it had to be ratified by conventions in at least nine states. By January of 1788, state conventions in Delaware, Pennsylvania, New Jersey, Georgia, and Connecticut had quickly given the new Constitution their seals of approval by wide margins. However, the Massachusetts convention, which ratified the Constitution by a narrow margin of 187–168, foreshadowed a hard road to ratification. Massachusetts ratified the new Constitution on the condition that it would be amended by adding a bill of rights to limit the powers of the new federal government. As states continued to convene ratifying conventions, battle lines were drawn between the Federalists, who supported ratification, and the Antifederalists, who opposed ratification.

VIRGINIA AND NEW YORK

On June 21, 1788, New Hampshire became the ninth state to ratify the Constitution, making the Constitution official in those nine states. However, the populous states of Virginia and New York still stood as remaining roadblocks to ratification. Virginia's ratifying convention was a tumultuous affair that was dominated by the opposition of the great revolutionary orator Patrick Henry. The Virginians narrowly favored ratification by a vote of 89–79 on the condition that twenty amendments be made to the document.

After Virginia, all eyes were on New York, where a great debate had been raging in the press for some time between Federalist and

Antifederalist writers. Most of these writers used Greco-Roman pseudonyms so readers would focus solely on their arguments. One of the most prominent Antifederalists wrote as "Brutus" (after the Roman politician who led the plot to assassinate Julius Caesar). Brutus argued that the Constitution sought to set up a national government rather than a federal union of states. He argued that large republics were fragile, making it easy for a small group of politicians to undermine the will of the people, resulting in rule by an aristocratic elite. He also believed that it was impossible for members of Congress to "know the minds of their constituents" when these constituents came from states spanning from New Hampshire to Georgia. Brutus also saw the creation of a federal judiciary as a danger, believing that the day would come when federal courts would "eclipse the dignity...of the state courts."

> In a free republic, although all laws are derived from the consent of the people, yet the people do not declare their consent by themselves in person, but by representatives, chosen by them, who are supposed to know the minds of their constituents, and to be possessed of integrity to declare this mind.
>
> —Brutus No. 1

Many Antifederalists saw the Constitution as a threat to both federalism and republicanism, believing that a government under the Constitution would undermine the rights of the states and make it impossible for the people to control their government. However, some Antifederalists believed that the Constitution was not inherently dangerous, but that it needed a bill of rights to guarantee the rights of the people and the states.

THE FEDERALIST PAPERS

Supporters of the Constitution feared that Antifederalist writers could prevent New York from ratifying the proposed Constitution. So, in defense of the Constitution, Alexander Hamilton recruited John Jay and James Madison to help him defend the Constitution with a series of essays known today as *The Federalist Papers*. John Jay became ill early in the writing process, so *The Federalist Papers* were largely a collaboration between Hamilton and Madison. Hamilton, Madison, and Jay chose the pseudonym "Publius," after Publius Valerius, the "people's friend," who had saved the Roman Republic in its infancy. The eighty-five essays of *The Federalist Papers* presented arguments in favor of the ratification of the Constitution, assuring the people of New York that it conformed with both federal and republican principles.

A Propaganda Campaign

The Federalist Papers were not written primarily to explain the Constitution's meaning but also to persuade New Yorkers to ratify it. Despite their persuasive purpose, *The Federalist Papers* remain a valuable source today for those who seek to understand what the framers of the Constitution intended when writing the Constitution.

By calling themselves Federalists, supporters of the Constitution gained a rhetorical victory, positioning themselves as proponents of a strong federal government that would preserve many powers of the states. Furthermore, by referring to their opponents as

Antifederalists, they were able to portray those who opposed ratification as opposing any union of the states whatsoever.

The New York ratifying convention ratified the Constitution by a narrow vote of 30–27. However, the New York convention also proposed amendments to the Constitution to protect the rights of the states and the people. With this in mind, ratification was more of a compromise between the Federalists and Antifederalists rather than an outright victory for the Federalists. In Federalist No. 84, Hamilton argued passionately against adding a bill of rights to the Constitution, claiming that it was a relic of the British monarchy. Privately, however, Hamilton feared that a bill of rights would undo much of the progress made by the Constitutional Convention in creating a strong central government. So, while the Antifederalists were unsuccessful in preventing ratification, the Federalists were also unsuccessful in their efforts to ratify the original Constitution.

James Madison proved more flexible than Hamilton, taking it upon himself to draft the amendments to the Constitution that would become known as the Bill of Rights. The first ten amendments that make up the Bill of Rights were ratified by the states in 1791, only three years after the ratification of the Constitution.

A STRONG CENTRAL GOVERNMENT

Nationalizing Features of the Constitution

"There is scarcely anything that can wound the pride or degrade the character of an independent nation which we do not experience," Alexander Hamilton wrote in Federalist No. 15, underscoring his point that the United States had reached the "last stage of national humiliation" under the Articles. Hamilton cited the continued presence of British forts on the border with Canada, failed attempts to negotiate free navigation of the Mississippi River from Spain, and a mountain of unpaid debts as evidence that the United States needed a strong central government. The Constitution strengthened the central government by giving the federal government new economic powers, a unitary executive, and an independent judiciary.

NEW ECONOMIC POWERS

The Constitution delegated new economic powers to Congress that had been absent under the Articles. Article I, Section 8 of the Constitution grants Congress the power to collect taxes on imports as well as to collect internal taxes equally throughout the states. The taxing power guaranteed that the federal government would be able to fund its operations (which had been problematic under the Articles). In addition to the power to tax imports, the Commerce Clause gave Congress the power to regulate all foreign trade as well as interstate commerce (goods moving from state to state). Under the Constitution, the states delegated away all powers to tax foreign trade and goods entering their states from other states. However, the states retained the power to tax their own citizens and kept control over all commerce that took place within a single state. This division of economic powers demonstrates the Constitution's commitment to maintaining federalism while increasing the powers of the central government.

A UNITARY EXECUTIVE

An executive branch led by a single chief executive was one of the greatest achievements of the Federalists, as the presidency had been a target of Antifederalist critics. "Wherein does this president...essentially differ from the king of Great Britain?" asked an Antifederalist writing under the pseudonym "Cato." There was skepticism about investing one person with the power to administer the entire executive branch. Alexander Hamilton, however, argued in Federalist No. 70 that a unitary executive was the only way the government could have the necessary "energy" needed to accomplish its day-to-day tasks.

> Energy in the Executive is a leading character in the definition of good government. It is essential to the protection of the community against foreign attacks; it is not less essential to the steady administration of the laws; to the protection of property...to the security of liberty against the enterprises and assaults of ambition, of faction, and of anarchy.
>
> —Federalist No. 70

Under the Articles, the executive functions of the government were carried out by an executive committee that had no independence from Congress. The Constitution provides for a single executive who can respond quickly and make important decisions in times of crisis.

THE FEDERAL JUDICIARY

Throughout American history, the federal judiciary has become an increasingly powerful pillar of the government, and it has often favored the expansion of federal authority. However, at the time, few foresaw the impact that the federal judiciary would make. In Federalist No. 78, Alexander Hamilton predicted that the judicial branch would be "the least dangerous to the political rights of the Constitution." He also argued in defense of the judiciary's existence as an unelected branch, claiming that not having to stand for elections would make federal judges more impartial in their rulings.

A LARGE REPUBLIC

The Constitution transformed the United States from a loose confederation of thirteen sovereign republics to a union of states that could also be spoken of as a single republic. Antifederalist writers had warned that strengthening the powers of the federal government was a threat to liberty, but Madison saw greater threats to liberty at work in the state governments—many of which had fallen under the control of a single political faction. Madison wrote:

The influence of factious leaders may kindle a flame within their particular States, but will be unable to spread a general conflagration through the other States. A religious sect may degenerate into a political faction in a part of the Confederacy; but the variety of sects dispersed over the entire face of it must secure the national councils against any danger from that source.

—Federalist No. 10

Political factions will always exist as long as there are elections, but the more populous a republic, the more difficult it will become for a single faction to take control of the government. Consider how common it is for one political party to control a state's governorship and legislature compared to how often a party can do the same thing at the federal level. The larger the republic, the greater the diversity of constituencies that elect representatives to Congress.

PARTLY NATIONAL, PARTLY FEDERAL

Although the Constitution granted the federal government new economic powers, created new branches of government, and inched the United States closer to nationhood, the federal core of the Articles was not entirely abandoned. In Federalist No. 39, Madison refuted Antifederalist claims that the Constitution created a national government by examining both its national and federal features. He concluded that the Constitution was "neither a national nor a federal Constitution, but a composition of both." In creating a government with both national and federal aspects, the framers of the Constitution steered into uncharted waters.

CHECKS AND BALANCES

Preventing Tyranny with Enlightenment Principles

In the face of relentless criticism from Antifederalists, the Federalists expressed confidence that the government created by the Constitution would not turn into a tyrannical regime. This confidence was rooted in the framers' faith in the principles of the Enlightenment. The Constitution had been carefully crafted not only to separate the legislative, executive, and judicial powers of the government but also to give each branch the power to check and balance the others. Since the framers instilled a healthy rivalry among the branches, the government would find itself unable to act unless supported by a broad consensus.

THE INFLUENCE OF THE ENLIGHTENMENT

The framers were heavily influenced by the philosophers of the Enlightenment, a European intellectual movement that occurred in the eighteenth century. Enlightenment philosophers believed that scientific principles could be applied to make governments that protected people's liberties. Instead of focusing on royal legitimacy based on hereditary succession, Enlightenment philosophers such as John Locke and Montesquieu argued that governments should be organized on a more rational basis.

John Locke

John Locke was an English philosopher who argued that governments exist primarily to protect the natural rights of life, liberty, and property. Locke advocated for religious toleration, influencing the Constitution's stance on religious freedom. While Locke's influence is most clear in the Declaration of Independence, he also inspired the Constitution's protection of property and civil liberties.

Montesquieu

Charles Louis de Secondat, Baron de Montesquieu, was a French nobleman who published *The Spirit of the Laws*, a treatise on political philosophy, in 1748. Montesquieu categorized governments into three types: despotic, feudal, and republican. He argued that the primary principle that separated republics from despotic (arbitrary) governments was the separation of powers. A republican form of government separates the legislative (lawmaking), executive (enforcing), and judicial (judging) powers of the government into different branches. Montesquieu illustrated these principles by making extensive comparisons between the ancient Roman Republic and the French absolute monarchy of his own time.

Montesquieu praised the Roman Republic, which separated government power into three branches and gave each branch checks against the others. He believed that a system of checks and balances among the branches was key to preserving the liberties of the people in a republican government. For example, Roman consuls had the power to command the armies, but only the Senate could decide where those armies would be sent.

MADISON AND FEDERALIST 51

Of the eighty-five essays in *The Federalist Papers*, none is more memorable in its explanation of checks and balances than James Madison's Federalist No. 51, in which he argues that the Constitution's built-in system of checks and balances would preserve liberty and a republican government. Although the Constitution gave the federal government new powers, checks and balances among the three branches would prevent these powers from transforming into a tyrannical regime.

If Men Were Angels

If men were angels, no government would be necessary. If angels were to govern men, neither external nor internal controls on government would be necessary. In framing a government which is to be administered by men over men, the great difficulty lies in this: you must first enable the government to control the governed; and in the next place oblige it to control itself.

—Federalist No. 51 (Madison)

In his eloquent comparison of men and angels, Madison demonstrated his awareness of the risks that came with giving the federal government new powers. Indeed, the framers inserted several checks and balances to enable officers of the government to check the operations of the other branches in a spirit of rivalry. In this sense, Madison's principle that "ambition must be made to counteract ambition" would keep the Constitution's government from ever being a threat to the people's liberties.

EXAMPLES OF CHECKS AND BALANCES

The Constitution contains several checks and balances to ensure that none of the branches of government can gain a decisive advantage over the others. The most prominent checks include a bicameral legislature, the presidential veto, and the judicial confirmation process.

A Bicameral Legislature

According to Madison, the establishment of a bicameral legislature included the benefit of making it more difficult to pass legislation than it had been under the unicameral Congress established by the Articles. Only a bill found acceptable to both the Senate and the House could become law. This represents an internal check within the legislative branch.

The Presidential Veto

The Constitution gives the president the power to veto legislation passed by Congress, inserting the chief executive into the legislative process. While the president's veto is not absolute (a two-thirds majority of both the Senate and the House can override a presidential veto), only about 10 percent of presidential vetoes are overridden by Congress.

Nominations and Confirmations

All federal judges, cabinet officials, and foreign ambassadors must be nominated by the president and confirmed by the Senate. This means that there must be a consensus between two branches of government before executive officials and federal judges are allowed to exercise authority.

Federalism

In Federalist No. 51, Madison stated that even if the system of checks and balances failed at the federal level, the federal structure of the government would give the states the power to intervene. Although this maneuver has never been employed, the Constitution grants the states the power to circumvent Congress and call a convention to propose constitutional amendments.

ASPIRATIONS OF THE PREAMBLE

A Vision for a More Perfect Union

The Preamble to the Constitution is arguably the most well-known and familiar part of the entire document. Generations of American schoolchildren have grown up memorizing the Preamble in their elementary school classes. "We the People" is stamped next to the face of Alexander Hamilton on the ten-dollar bill. The Preamble's language does not carry legal weight, but it is much more than a paragraph of well-written words cleverly woven together. The Preamble declares the ways in which the Constitution provides continuity with and improvement upon the Articles of Confederation.

Although the Preamble comes first in the Constitution, it was one of the last portions to be written. The language, largely credited to Pennsylvania delegate Gouverneur Morris, was never debated at any point by the convention delegates. Each phrase of the Preamble makes its own statement about the Constitution's authority and purpose.

> We the People of the United States, in Order to form a more perfect Union, establish Justice, insure domestic Tranquility, provide for the common defence, promote the general Welfare, and secure the Blessings of Liberty to ourselves and our Posterity, do ordain and establish this Constitution for the United States of America.
>
> —The Constitution, Preamble

WE THE PEOPLE

The Constitution begins by establishing that its authority comes from "the people," not a monarch. "The People of the United States" is an interesting phrase, as the Constitution does not list the states by name. While some have claimed that the framers intended the Constitution to create a national (not federal) government, the text of the Constitution clearly establishes that the states retain many of their sovereign powers. It is more likely that naming each state in the Preamble would have been cumbersome. Plus, no one knew for sure how many states (or which states) would ratify the Constitution.

A MORE PERFECT UNION

The framers of the Constitution believed that their plan of government was superior to that of the Articles. While the Articles declared that the states were in a "firm league of friendship," the Constitution likens states' relationships to marriage. The delegates to the Constitutional Convention hoped that their plan of government would last longer, work more effectively, and unite the American people more than the Articles had.

ESTABLISH JUSTICE

Under the Articles of Confederation, there was no federal court system. This made it extremely difficult to settle legal disputes between two states or between residents of different states. The federal court system established by the Constitution filled many of the important gaps facing the American legal system under the Articles.

INSURE DOMESTIC TRANQUILITY

Shays' Rebellion was the most likely inspiration for the phrase "insure domestic Tranquility." Governments are responsible for making sure people feel safe and that their property is protected. The Articles of Confederation had vested police power exclusively in the hands of state governments. However, the Constitution makes clear that maintaining internal peace is a shared responsibility between the states and the federal government.

PROVIDE FOR THE COMMON DEFENSE

Providing for the common defense was, essentially, the reason that states fought in the American Revolution and adopted the Articles of Confederation. This portion of the Preamble is one of its greatest expressions of continuity with the Articles. Note that the Preamble's use of "defence" is not a misspelling but is consistent with its British spelling. Plus, oddly enough, "defence" is the only noun in the Preamble that is not capitalized.

PROMOTE THE GENERAL WELFARE

In the Articles of Confederation, "mutual and general welfare" is one of the reasons that the states were entering into a federal arrangement together. The promotion of the general welfare (or the common good) of Americans is one of the central purposes of the federal government. Legally, this clause can be problematic, as one judge's idea of the common good can be much different than another's.

SECURE THE BLESSINGS OF LIBERTY

Again, the Articles of Confederation cited "the security of their Liberties" as one of the reasons the states were entering into a federal union. However, the Preamble extends this to include the words "to ourselves and our Posterity," indicating that they intended for this "more perfect Union" to preserve freedom for generations to come. They succeeded; today, the US Constitution is the world's oldest functioning written constitution.

THE STRUCTURE OF THE CONSTITUTION

Organizing a Tripartite Federal Government

One of the most basic functions of a constitution is the organization of a government, and it follows that the government's founding document should be organized too. While the Articles of Confederation created a federal union with only Congress administering it, the government created by the Constitution is not only federal in its structure; it is also tripartite (made up of three branches). The added complexity of the government created by the Constitution necessitates a governing document that is logical and well organized. The Constitution is organized into articles that detail the powers of the legislative, executive, and judicial branches of government. Each of these articles is subdivided into sections and clauses for easy reference.

ARTICLES, SECTIONS, AND CLAUSES

The largest section of the Constitution is called an article. The first three Articles of the Constitution detail the organization and powers of the three branches of government. Articles of the Constitution are represented by Roman numerals, which were commonly used at the time to organize official documents. Since the basis of a republican form of government is representation, Article I focuses on the legislative branch. This article details the structure and powers of both houses of Congress as well as how members of Congress are elected and the length of their terms.

After laws are made, they must be enforced, which is why Article II focuses on the presidency. Article II provides details concerning the president's powers, the length of the president's term, and the processes for electing and impeaching the president.

Article III establishes the federal judiciary and details the types of cases that fall under its jurisdiction. Articles IV through VII of the Constitution focus on relations among the states, amending the Constitution, the Constitution's authority, and the ratification of the Constitution, respectively.

Since the first four Articles of the Constitution are lengthy, these articles are divided into sections for easy reference. One of the most important sections of the Constitution is Article I, Section 8, which enumerates (lists) the powers of Congress. Someone wishing to run for Congress would go to Article I, Section 3 to see the qualifications for members of Congress, while someone curious about the powers of the president would consult Article II, Section 2. Unlike the articles, the sections are always represented by standard Arabic numerals.

Clauses are the smallest organizational units in the Constitution, used for referencing specific powers granted to the government by the Constitution or specific rights of the people that it protects. For example, the Commerce Clause can be found by going to Article I, Section 8, Clause 3, meaning that it is the third enumerated power delegated to Congress in Article I, Section 8. In some cases, a clause can form only a portion of a sentence. Take the First Amendment, for example:

Congress shall make no law respecting an establishment of religion, or prohibiting the free exercise thereof; or abridging the freedom of speech, or of the press; or the right of the people peaceably to assemble, and to petition the Government for a redress of grievances.

—The First Amendment of the Constitution

The First Amendment packs six clauses into a single sentence, protecting the rights of citizens to freely express themselves through religion, speech, the press, peaceful assembly, and petitions. Each of these miniature clauses is the subject of several Supreme Court decisions that clarify the extent and the limitations of each of these rights.

AMENDMENTS TO THE CONSTITUTION

The original text of the Constitution is followed by twenty-seven amendments. Some of these amendments have their own sections and clauses, while others are short and simple enough to have only one clause. The first ten amendments to the Constitution, known as the Bill of Rights, were ratified by the states shortly after the ratification of the Constitution. Each of these first ten amendments limits the powers of the federal government by protecting specific rights of the people and the states. From time to time, the Constitution has been amended in order to modernize it. Some of these amendments are purely procedural, such as the Twelfth Amendment, which altered the formula for selecting the vice president after the original method didn't work. At other times, amendments brought major social changes, such as the Nineteenth Amendment's prohibition of voter discrimination against women.

However significant an amendment may be in altering the Constitution, no amendment has ever been made to the Constitution's original text. Amendments are simply added to the Constitution after their passage. For example, although the Thirteenth Amendment, which outlaws slavery throughout the United States, rendered a number of clauses in the original Constitution (such as the Three-Fifths Compromise) to be void, these clauses have never been formally stricken from the Constitution.

Reading the Constitution

In 2011, the 112th Congress decided to begin its legislative session by reading the entire Constitution aloud. However, it used a version of the Constitution that removed obsolete clauses in order to avoid reading aloud the original Constitution's protections of slavery. This sparked some discussion about whether or not an oral reading of the Constitution should include these clauses.

INTERPRETING THE CONSTITUTION

Assigning Meaning to Written Words

While the framers may have known what they meant when they drafted the Constitution, they left behind 4,543 words that are subject to interpretation. There is some difficulty in interpreting a document that was written over two hundred years ago. Each person's interpretation of the document will be slightly different. Just as Americans had differing opinions about the Constitution during the debates over ratification, Americans today continue to have spirited and healthy debates about how best to determine the Constitution's meaning.

METHODS OF CONSTITUTIONAL INTERPRETATION

Anyone seeking to interpret the Constitution can choose from several schools of constitutional interpretation to guide them in deriving meaning from the document. These methods of interpretation differ in their ideas about the amount of power the Constitution gives to the federal government, how the text of the Constitution should be analyzed, and to what extent the Constitution should be understood to change with the times. In addition, judges have to decide how much to defer to the framers and how much to use their own judgment in deciding disputes about the law.

Strict and Loose Constructionism

Ever since the Founding Fathers' generation, politicians have debated whether to interpret the Constitution strictly or loosely. Strict constructionists, such as Thomas Jefferson, argued that the Constitution only gives the federal government the powers that are specifically enumerated within it. This would limit the powers of Congress to those listed in Article I, Section 8. Loose constructionists, such as Alexander Hamilton, believed that the Constitution was written as a general guideline for the federal government to follow—not an exhaustive listing of all of its powers. Loose constructionists believe that the Constitution's enumeration of certain powers also implies that the government can operate generally within the enumerated spheres. An example of this is the argument that Congress's power to coin and borrow money gives Congress a general license to operate within the financial sector.

Living Constitutionalism

Some jurists argue that the Constitution should be treated like a "living document," allowing its meaning to naturally evolve and change with the times. Living constitutionalists contend that this is the only way that a plan of government written over two hundred years ago can remain relevant to an ever-changing society. For example, the idea of "commerce" has changed quite a bit from the limited state-to-state trade of the eighteenth century to today's economy, in which many business transactions cross state lines. Living constitutionalists argue that judges should consider societal changes when making decisions, while opponents of this philosophy argue that it gives judges too much power at the expense of the democratically elected branches.

Judicial Activism versus Judicial Restraint

Advocates of a "living" Constitution tend to favor judicial activism, a judicial philosophy that encourages judges to incorporate their moral understandings into rulings. Supreme Court Justice Thurgood Marshall once replied when asked about his personal judicial philosophy: "You do what you think is right and let the law catch up." Marshall's philosophy was informed by his long career challenging segregation laws as an attorney for the National Association for the Advancement of Colored People.

Judges who favor judicial restraint attempt to base their rulings on the Constitution itself rather than on their opinions and morals. They believe that judges who consciously incorporate their opinions into their rulings circumvent the Constitution's formal amendment process, which gives this right to Congress and the states. Ultimately, in their view, basing judicial rulings on the original intent of the framers or the plain meaning of the Constitution's language results in a "government of laws and not of men."

Liberal and Conservative

Americans often describe judges as liberal or conservative, but these categories are highly subjective. While judicial conservatives tend to favor judicial restraint, they each have varying definitions of what that means. Although these terms can be useful, they can also muddy the waters sometimes since they primarily describe politicians rather than judges.

Originalism

Originalism is a specific form of judicial restraint that considers the original intent of the framers when it comes to court cases. An originalist, for example, would not believe that the Fourteenth

Amendment's Equal Protection Clause should be used to protect the right to same-sex marriages since, in the 1860s, marriage was defined as a contract between a man and a woman.

Critics of originalism often point to the controversial *Dred Scott v. Sandford* (1857) decision, in which the Supreme Court ruled that people of African descent could not be US citizens, citing its ruling not on the language of the Constitution but on what the justices believed the framers intended. The Constitution's text never connects citizenship with race. The *Dred Scott* ruling is an example of how originalism can become its own vehicle for judicial activism.

Textualism

Textualism is another form of judicial restraint. Textualists differ from originalists because they search *only* for the plain meaning of the Constitution's text. Advocates believe that their approach removes the subjectivity that comes with originalism. However, there are some disputes within the textualist camp regarding the exact method used to interpret a text.

The rift between textualists was quite evident in the Supreme Court's *Bostock v. Clayton County* (2020), in which Justice Neil Gorsuch wrote that Title VII of the Civil Rights Act of 1964 protects Americans from discrimination based on sexual orientation or gender identity, citing the law's prohibition of discrimination based on "sex." Conservative critics claimed that discrimination based on sex wasn't understood in 1964 to incorporate LGBT+ rights. Gorsuch, however, claimed that firing a man for being attracted to men is unjust since a heterosexual woman wouldn't be fired under the same circumstances. The *Bostock* decision sparked a debate between textualists, showing that the textualist approach is far from an exact science.

Chapter 2

The Protection of Rights

The Constitution provides an organizational structure for the federal government, outlines its powers, and protects the rights of Americans. Of these three functions of the Constitution, the protection of rights is the most impactful to everyday citizens. These constitutional rights are largely protected by amendments that were added after ratification. When Americans speak of their constitutional rights, they are generally referring to either the Bill of Rights (the first ten amendments) or the Fourteenth Amendment. It is time to examine how these constitutional amendments protect Americans' civil liberties and guarantee that civil rights are protected equally under the law.

THE BILL OF RIGHTS

The Protection of Civil Liberties

After the Constitution was ratified, James Madison studied the plethora of proposals submitted by Antifederalists at state ratifying conventions and found a common thread: The Constitution needed to clearly define the rights of the people. Madison then submitted several proposed amendments to Congress, twelve of which Congress sent to the states for ratification, and ten of which were quickly ratified by the states to become known as the Bill of Rights. The Bill of Rights, which protects the basic rights of all Americans, has a rich history that is worth exploring.

THE IDEA OF A BILL OF RIGHTS

The Bill of Rights had historical precedents from England, which inspired the Founding Fathers' ideas of constitutional rights. The Magna Carta, signed in 1215, represented an agreement between the English monarchy and feudal nobility about basic rights, such as the right to consent to taxation. The English Bill of Rights, which was influenced by John Locke's ideas, went further in guaranteeing the rights of English subjects, including protections against "cruel and unusual punishments" and the rights of law-abiding citizens (excluding Catholics) to bear "arms for their defense."

Following the Declaration of Independence, most states included bills of rights as preambles to their state constitutions. The most famous of these was the Virginia Declaration of Rights, written principally by George Mason (one of three delegates from the Constitutional Convention who refused to sign). Mason is known as the father of the bill of rights because of his authorship of the Virginia Declaration of Rights and his insistence that the Constitution needed a bill of rights.

Antifederalists insisted on including a bill of rights in the Constitution even though the Articles of Confederation did not include one. They believed this was necessary because the Constitution, unlike the Articles, represented a union of both the states and the American people.

A Preamble to the Preamble?

One of Madison's many proposals to Congress was for language to be added to the beginning of the Preamble in the form of "a declaration, that all power is originally vested in, and consequently derived from, the people." Had Madison's idea gained traction, the Constitution would not begin with "We the People."

THE BILL OF RIGHTS

The Bill of Rights includes the first ten amendments to the Constitution. Each amendment protects one right (or a category of rights) reserved for the states and the people.

- **Amendment I** guarantees the rights of freedom of expression, including freedom of religion, speech, the press, peaceful assembly, and petition.
- **Amendment II** protects the rights of Americans to keep and bear arms for their own defense and for citizen participation in state militias to protect against foreign invasion.
- **Amendment III** forbids the federal government from quartering soldiers in private homes and buildings during peacetime without the owner's consent. Largely a protest against the British

colonial practice of housing soldiers in private buildings, the Third Amendment has caused little controversy since its ratification and has never been the subject of a Supreme Court case.

- **Amendment IV** protects Americans against unreasonable searches and seizures, forbidding government officials from conducting unwarranted searches of private property.
- **Amendment V** addresses criminal procedure, protecting Americans from double jeopardy (being tried twice for a single crime) and self-incrimination (testifying as a witness against oneself). The Fifth Amendment's Due Process Clause guarantees that Americans will not "be deprived of life, liberty, or property, without due process of law."
- **Amendment VI** clarifies criminal trial procedures, promising every American "a speedy and public trial" in the state where the alleged crime was committed. Americans who face criminal charges are guaranteed legal counsel from an attorney, the right to call witnesses on their behalf, and the right to confront witnesses who give testimony against them.
- **Amendment VII** guarantees Americans the right to a jury in civil trials. These are lawsuits where the defendant is not accused of a crime but is alleged to be liable for damages or monetary losses suffered by another party.
- **Amendment VIII** protects Americans who are found guilty of criminal acts from excessive fines and bails, as well as from "cruel and unusual punishments."
- **Amendment IX** clarifies that the enumeration of the people's rights in the Bill of Rights is not intended to be fully comprehensive and that the people retain other rights beyond these.
- **Amendment X** asserts that the states, as well as the people, retain all rights and powers that are not delegated to the federal government by the Constitution.

JUDICIAL REVIEW

Deciding What the Constitution Says

The Bill of Rights may seem clear in its enumeration of the rights of Americans. But what happens when people read these amendments in a different way? There are many ways to interpret the Constitution, and not everyone understands it in the same way. Ultimately, someone has to decide on an interpretation, but the Constitution doesn't spell out who gets to make these important decisions. The Supreme Court has assumed this role. Judicial review is the term signifying the Court's power to decide what the Constitution means.

JUDICIAL REVIEW IN THE UNITED STATES

The Supreme Court's power of judicial review is actually never explicitly defined in the text of the Constitution. However, it was agreed that someone had to intervene when Congress passed laws that went beyond its powers under the Constitution. Two explanations were offered concerning how a law that ran counter to the Constitution might be voided.

Compact Theory

Thomas Jefferson and James Madison advocated for the compact theory of the Constitution. According to compact theory, the Constitution is a binding contract between the states, and the states have the ultimate authority to decide when federal legislation violates the Constitution. While Madison supported the idea of the states challenging a federal law together, Jefferson asserted that an individual state might nullify (reject) an unconstitutional federal law by refusing to enforce it within its borders. Although compact theory had its share of early supporters, the Supreme Court's *Marbury v. Madison* decision has had a more lasting impact.

Marbury v. Madison

In 1800, Thomas Jefferson was elected president in an election that he and his supporters called the "Revolution of 1800." When Jefferson took office, he and his right-hand man, Secretary of State James Madison, had to decide what to do with undelivered judicial commissions left by John Adams's administration. Having defeated Adams in a hotly contested election, Jefferson instructed Madison not to deliver the commissions, which would have given federal judgeships to their political opponents. One of these judges was William Marbury, who was unhappy to learn that he would not be receiving the commission that President Adams had promised.

Marbury took his complaint directly to the Supreme Court on the basis of Section 13 of the Judiciary Act of 1789. This act gave the Court original jurisdiction (the authority to be the first court to hear a case) in cases involving writs of mandamus. A writ of mandamus is a court order to a government official requiring the official to take a specific action. Chief Justice John Marshall, who had been John Adams's secretary of state, was placed in a difficult position because Madison, as a member of the executive branch, might have been inclined to ignore a writ of mandamus from the Court, which had no power to enforce it.

Chief Justice Marshall, always the clever legal thinker, decided to sidestep the issue between Marbury and Madison, choosing instead to rule on the constitutionality of the Judiciary Act of 1789, which gave the Supreme Court a very limited sphere of original jurisdiction over cases in which a state or foreign ambassador was a party. In *Marbury v. Madison* (1803), the Court ruled Section 13 of the Judiciary Act of 1789 to be unconstitutional and therefore void. In the opinion of the Court, Marshall asserted the Supreme Court's right to have the final word in disputes concerning the Constitution.

> It is emphatically the province and duty of the judicial department to say what the law is....If two laws conflict with each other, the courts must decide on the operation of each.
>
> —John Marshall, *Marbury v. Madison* (1803)

The *Marbury v. Madison* ruling is often considered to be the most significant Supreme Court decision ever made, as the Court now claimed the power to strike down laws (or portions of laws) that conflicted with the Constitution.

Interchangeable Terms

When reading about the Supreme Court, the words *decision*, *ruling*, and *holding* come up often. These terms all describe the same thing: the judgment of the Court in favor of one party or the other in a legal case.

JUDICIAL OPINIONS

The Supreme Court's decisions are not handed down without explanation. These decisions are accompanied by judicial opinions, in which the justices explain their reasoning. Some justices disagree with the Court's decision; others may agree with the decision but have a different rationale for reaching the same conclusion. Each justice may present their opinion on any decision in a number of ways.

Majority Opinion

The majority opinion serves as the official opinion of the Court and is written by one justice who is joined by the majority. Since the Supreme Court has nine justices, it takes at least five justices' signatures to make it the majority opinion.

Concurring Opinion

A justice writes a concurring opinion to express agreement with the opinion of the Court but also to explain their own separate reasoning process in arriving at the same decision. It is permissible for a justice to sign the majority opinion and contribute a concurring opinion. In complex court rulings, a concurring opinion may only agree with a portion of the ruling and disagrees with (or dissents from) most aspects of the majority opinion.

Dissenting Opinion

A dissenting opinion expresses the disagreement of one or more justices with the Court's decision. Although dissenting opinions have no official legal weight, they can be extremely useful when the Court is considering overturning a decision, as it did when *Brown v. Board of Education* (1954) overturned the *Plessy v. Ferguson* (1896) decision.

EQUAL PROTECTION OF THE LAWS

The Game-Changing Fourteenth Amendment

When the Constitution was ratified, Americans were concerned that the new federal government established by the Constitution would become a threat to the rights of the people and the states. However, the American Civil War (1861–1865) prompted Americans to reevaluate the relationship between the states and the federal government. Congressional Republicans (with a large majority in both houses) wanted the federal government to protect the rights of Americans from state governments that would deny citizenship and basic rights to entire classes of citizens (in this case, Black people in the South). The desire for the federal government's involvement in guaranteeing civil rights culminated in the ratification of the Fourteenth Amendment, which guarantees the rights of citizenship, due process, and equal protection of the laws to all native-born and naturalized Americans.

UNDERSTANDING THE FOURTEENTH AMENDMENT

After the ratification of the Thirteenth Amendment, which abolished slavery in the United States, the legal status of recently freed men and women in the South was uncertain. The Supreme Court's *Dred Scott* decision had ruled out granting citizenship to African Americans, and no rule in the Constitution expressly prohibited states from treating formerly enslaved people as something less than citizens.

Several Southern states passed "Black Codes," which restricted the civil liberties of African Americans, denying them basic rights, such as bearing arms and forming religious associations without a permit from the state. The Fourteenth Amendment was drafted in response, granting them the benefits of full citizenship.

The Fourteenth Amendment is the longest and most complex of all of the constitutional amendments. While most amendments were drafted with a single objective in mind, the Fourteenth Amendment sought to fundamentally redefine citizenship, expand civil rights protections, and alter the relationship between the federal and state governments. Its most significant clauses, which have been the subject of landmark Supreme Court cases, are in Section 1.

> All persons born or naturalized in the United States, and subject to the jurisdiction thereof, are citizens of the United States and of the State wherein they reside. No State shall make or enforce any law which shall abridge the privileges or immunities of citizens of the United States; nor shall any State deprive any person of life, liberty, or property, without due process of law; nor deny to any person within its jurisdiction the equal protection of the laws.
> —Section 1, Fourteenth Amendment of the Constitution

SIGNIFICANT CLAUSES

The most significant clauses of the Fourteenth Amendment are the Citizenship Clause, the Privileges or Immunities Clause, the Due Process Clause, and the Equal Protection Clause.

Citizenship Clause

The Fourteenth Amendment's Citizenship Clause confers citizenship upon everyone born in the United States. When the Fourteenth Amendment was ratified, granting birthright citizenship regardless of the citizenship status of the parents was rare, but it guaranteed that African Americans in the South would have equal rights. Although birthright citizenship is normal in the Americas today, few other nations grant this citizenship when neither parent is a citizen of the country.

Privileges or Immunities Clause

Article IV of the original Constitution contains a Privileges *and* Immunities Clause which reads: "The Citizens of each State shall be entitled to all Privileges and Immunities of Citizens in the several States," but there was no language to enforce this. Citizenship is understood to come with privileges, like voting rights and the right to free speech, and immunities, like protections from cruel and unusual punishments. The framers of the Fourteenth Amendment wanted to clarify that all Americans are entitled to these rights and that Congress (according to Section 5 of the Fourteenth Amendment) may pass laws to protect the privileges and immunities of American citizens.

The Fourteenth Amendment's Privileges or Immunities Clause (not to be confused with the Privileges *and* Immunities Clause in the original Constitution) reads: "No State shall make or enforce any law which shall abridge the privileges or immunities of citizens of the United States." The inclusion of the phrase "No State shall" represents a remarkable turning point in the Constitution when compared to the Bill of Rights, which sought to limit the ability of the federal government to infringe upon the rights of Americans.

The Fourteenth Amendment places the same limitation on state governments.

Due Process Clause

The Fourteenth Amendment's Due Process Clause reads: "Nor shall any State deprive any person of life, liberty, or property, without due process of law." The Fifth Amendment specifically prevents the federal government from taking a person's life, liberty, or property without due process of law. The Fourteenth Amendment applies the restrictions at the state level.

Equal Protection Clause

The Fourteenth Amendment's Equal Protection Clause prohibits states from denying anyone "the equal protection of the laws." The Equal Protection Clause represents the first time that the Constitution required state governments to treat everyone equally under the law. The original Constitution, ratified when many states sanctioned slavery and required property ownership to vote, did not require state governments to treat all citizens equally. Famous court cases like *Brown v. Board of Education* (1954) were decided based on the Equal Protection Clause.

Subsequent Sections

While Section 1 of the Fourteenth Amendment is the most relevant to guaranteeing civil rights and due process to Americans, Sections 2, 3, and 4 of the Fourteenth Amendment address important matters of constitutional law, including discrimination in voting, disqualification for office holding, and the payment of the national debt.

THE INCORPORATION DOCTRINE

Applying the Bill of Rights to the States

Although the Fourteenth Amendment states that all Americans have a constitutional right to "equal protection of the laws," it does not clearly define which rights are included under the umbrella of equal protection. Similarly, the Fourteenth Amendment's prohibition on state seizures of life, liberty, or property without due process of law is ambiguous about the extent to which the process can differ from state to state. Requiring every state's justice system to be the same destroys the idea of federalism. However, equal protection and due process require some degree of standardization. Over the years, the Supreme Court has applied the incorporation doctrine to decide which of the provisions of the Bill of Rights are applicable to state governments.

WHAT IS THE INCORPORATION DOCTRINE?

The incorporation doctrine is the idea that the Fourteenth Amendment makes many of the provisions of the Bill of Rights binding on the states. The Supreme Court has chosen to incorporate specific provisions of the Bill of Rights selectively through decisions about individual cases. When using selective incorporation, the Court considers whether incorporation of a right is necessary for Americans to enjoy the Fourteenth Amendment's guarantee of due process rights and the equal protection of the laws.

Barron v. Baltimore (1833)

In an 1833 case, the Supreme Court rejected John Barron's claim that the city of Baltimore's construction projects had negatively impacted his business, depriving him of property without due process of law. In its unanimous ruling, the Court rejected Barron's claim that the Fifth Amendment's Due Process Clause applied to the states. Before the Fourteenth Amendment, the *Barron* case exempted the states from the Bill of Rights.

Incorporated Amendments

The Supreme Court has incorporated every clause of the First, Second, Fourth, and Eighth Amendments, and most of the Fifth and Sixth Amendments, as being binding on the states through the Fourteenth Amendment. The incorporation of the First Amendment began with *Gitlow v. New York* (1925), in which the Supreme Court provided guidelines by which the states could (and could not) regulate free speech. The *Gitlow* decision was the first time the Supreme Court incorporated freedom of speech and the press onto the states.

Over the years, the Supreme Court has incorporated most of the Bill of Rights' protections for criminal defendants as binding on the states. For example, *Gideon v. Wainwright* (1963) incorporated the right to an attorney for state criminal defendants, and in the controversial *Miranda v. Arizona* (1966) case, the Supreme Court ordered a retrial for Ernesto Miranda, who had confessed to rape before being informed of his right to remain silent.

The process of selective incorporation, which requires a case to be brought before the Supreme Court for a right to be incorporated, can sometimes create confusion. Before the landmark *District of Columbia v. Heller* (2008) decision, the Supreme Court had never ruled definitively on whether the Second Amendment protects an individual's right to bear arms or whether it only applied to individuals serving in a state militia. After the *Heller* decision, the Supreme Court took two more years to incorporate the Second Amendment into the states in *McDonald v. Chicago* (2010). Provisions of the Bill of Rights that have not yet been incorporated may be incorporated by a future Supreme Court ruling.

Total Incorporation

Some legal scholars have argued for the doctrine of total incorporation, which would incorporate every provision of the Bill of Rights as applicable to both federal and state governments. Although the Supreme Court rejected the doctrine of total incorporation, most of the provisions of the Bill of Rights have been incorporated as binding upon the states.

Unincorporated Amendments

The Supreme Court has never incorporated the Third, Seventh, Ninth, and Tenth Amendments to apply to the states. The Third Amendment has never been the subject of a case before the Supreme Court, and this is not likely to change. The Seventh Amendment's guarantee of a jury trial in federal civil cases has also not been incorporated, allowing states to determine when jury trials are legally necessary in civil cases.

Additionally, the Fifth Amendment has been partially incorporated, but states can decide whether or not to require that grand juries be convened to examine evidence prior to indicting someone with a crime. Similarly, states are not bound by the Sixth Amendment's requirement that juries be composed of people who reside in the locality where the alleged crime was committed. This enables state authorities to move a trial when there is doubt as to whether a local jury will administer impartial justice.

Although some efforts have been made to incorporate the Ninth Amendment (namely in cases involving a right to privacy), the Supreme Court has never done so, choosing instead to stick to incorporating rights that are specifically enumerated in the Bill of Rights. And, finally, because of the Tenth Amendment's purpose in protecting the rights of the states against federal overreach, it is difficult to imagine a scenario in which it would be incorporated.

FREEDOM OF RELIGION

The Establishment and Free Exercise Clauses

The first right protected in the Bill of Rights is freedom of religion. Although Article VI of the Constitution states that "no religious Test shall ever be required as a Qualification to any Office or public Trust under the United States," there is no language in the original Constitution that expressly prohibits the federal government from mandating religious expression, favoring one religion over another, or prohibiting the activities of a religious minority. The First Amendment solves this problem with two religion clauses that prevent the federal government from establishing a religion and preventing interference with the free exercise of religion.

THE DEVELOPMENT OF RELIGIOUS FREEDOM

The First Amendment's religion clauses are the result of a long history that began with religious persecution in England, continued with the expansion of religious toleration in the thirteen colonies, and ended with complete religious freedom after the American Revolution.

Religious Persecution in England

Religious freedom in America is rooted in England's storied history of religious disputes. In 1534, King Henry VIII renounced Catholicism and created the Anglican Church, a faith he forced on

all of his subjects. Over the next century, English monarchs perse-
cuted Catholics and other religious dissenters, including Puritans
and Quakers. Many journeyed to the colonies to escape religious
persecution.

Toleration in the Colonies

Each of the thirteen colonies developed their own distinct ideas
of religious toleration over time. Colonies in New England, such
as Massachusetts, established churches and punished religious
dissenters. Roger Williams, for example, was exiled for preaching
against any kind of religious coercion by government authorities.
Maryland, founded as a haven for Catholics, allowed all Christians
to settle there as long as they believed Jesus to be the Son of God by
the standard Trinitarian definition. However, it was a capital offense
in the Maryland Colony to deny the divinity of Jesus. William Penn,
who established the Pennsylvania Colony, established a policy of
full religious toleration in accordance with his Quaker beliefs. In
Georgia, only Catholicism was prohibited as a religion (the English
feared that Catholic colonists might join the Spanish if the colony
were invaded from neighboring Spanish Florida). By the time of the
American Revolution, most of the colonies practiced religious toleration while requiring colonists to support an established church
through taxes.

The Virginia Statute for Religious Freedom

Just over a year before the Constitutional Convention, the Vir-
ginia General Assembly approved the Virginia Statute for Religious
Freedom, authored by Thomas Jefferson. This act disestablished the
Anglican Church in Virginia, depriving it of any further tax support.
The Virginia Statute for Religious Freedom asserted that "our civil

rights have no dependence on our religious opinions, any more than our opinions in physics or geometry," expressing Jefferson's belief that everyone should be able to freely practice their religion.

> Congress shall make no law respecting an establishment of religion, or prohibiting the free exercise thereof.
>
> —Amendment I to the Constitution

As one can see, the First Amendment begins with two clauses concerning religion: the Establishment Clause and the Free Exercise Clause.

THE ESTABLISHMENT CLAUSE

The Establishment Clause prohibits the federal government from establishing a religion. People still debate the precise meaning of "establishing a religion," but it generally involves a government collecting taxes to support religious sects, showing favor toward one religion over another, or compelling participation in religious activities.

Incorporation of the Establishment Clause

The Supreme Court first incorporated the Establishment Clause to the states in *Everson v. Board of Education* (1947). Arch Everson believed that a law reimbursing parents for transportation expenses for public or religious schools violated the Establishment Clause. In a 5–4 ruling, the Court's narrow majority ruled that the New Jersey law did not violate the idea of a "wall of separation" between church and state because it gave every parent an equal right to reimbursement, regardless of school type. This case opened the door for the Court to incorporate the Establishment Clause onto the states.

A Wall of Separation

The metaphor of a "wall of separation" between church and state originated in a letter from Thomas Jefferson to the Danbury Baptist Association of Connecticut in 1802. The phrase has appeared in many Supreme Court opinions over the past century.

School Prayer

Engel v. Vitale (1962) was a landmark Supreme Court ruling that held school prayer to be a violation of the Establishment Clause. It involved a prayer that had been approved for use in New York schools each morning, asking for blessings from "Almighty God" without mentioning any specific belief or deity. The Court ruled that even a non-sectarian prayer during school was incompatible with the separation of church and state.

The *Engel* decision serves as a reminder that the Supreme Court is not as closely bound to public opinion as the elected branches. The ruling came at a time when a much higher percentage of Americans identified as religious (particularly as Christian) than today. As recently as 2014, a Gallup poll showed that a majority of Americans still express support for school prayer, though that majority is smaller than the 70 percent in 1999.

Civic Deism

The Establishment Clause doesn't prohibit the government or public officials from making generic supplications to God. When presidents conclude their speeches by saying, "God bless America," such language is generally interpreted as a generic desire for God's blessings. This practice, known as civic deism, is also seen in the

Pledge of Allegiance and on US currency, which is stamped with "In God We Trust."

Legislative Prayer

In *Town of Greece v. Galloway* (2014), the Supreme Court ruled that the common practice by legislative bodies of beginning their sessions with prayer by sectarian clergy does not violate the Establishment Clause if kept within certain limits. To align with the Constitution, legislative prayer must not compel anyone's participation, belittle any religious (or irreligious) group, or attempt to convert anyone.

THE FREE EXERCISE CLAUSE

While the Establishment Clause was designed to prohibit the government from endorsing a religious sect, it is balanced by the Free Exercise Clause, which protects the right of individuals and religious groups to practice their religions freely.

Incorporation of the Free Exercise Clause

The Supreme Court first incorporated the Free Exercise Clause in *Cantwell v. Connecticut* (1940), a unanimous decision in which the Court struck down a state law that discriminated against religious groups when granting solicitation permits. The Connecticut law resulted in the arrest of three Jehovah's Witnesses, who were charged with soliciting without a license. The Court ruled that a state cannot enact laws to stop Americans from freely preaching and spreading religious views.

Free Exercise and Parental Rights

The Free Exercise Clause also protects the rights of parents to raise their children within their chosen religious tradition. In *Wisconsin v. Yoder* (1972), the Supreme Court ruled in favor of Amish parents who pulled their children from public schools after finishing the eighth grade, which violated Wisconsin's state law requiring all students to attend school until the age of sixteen. Because the Amish parents cited their legitimate religious beliefs as a justification for not sending their children to high school, the Court ruled that the Wisconsin law violated the Free Exercise Clause because it did not include a religious exemption.

Voluntary Prayer in Schools

Although the Supreme Court has ruled against the constitutionality of prayer during the school day or at school functions, students may practice their religion during the school day, both individually and through faith-based clubs. In *Kennedy v. Bremerton School District* (2022), the Court upheld a football coach's right to pray at the fifty-yard line after games. What began as an individual prayer grew into a noticeable ritual, as players began to voluntarily join their coach. The Court held that by asking the coach to stop praying, the school district had violated his rights under the Free Exercise Clause.

FREEDOM OF SPEECH

The Constitution's Most Celebrated Right

Although freedom of speech is not the first to be listed in the First Amendment, it's the most widely recognized constitutional right. Because of the protections of the First Amendment, Americans have a nearly unbridled liberty to express their opinions about sensitive subjects, such as religion and politics, that would result in someone being imprisoned in many societies. Yet, in spite of such liberty afforded by the First Amendment, there are some cases in which speech can become a criminal offense.

THE FREE SPEECH CLAUSE

The Free Speech Clause states that "Congress shall make no law... abridging the freedom of speech." This clause prohibits Congress from passing laws that limit freedom of speech, although Congress has attempted to restrict speech by passing questionable laws in the past (especially during wartime). The Supreme Court has often been in the difficult position of balancing the government's prerogative to prevent its own overthrow with citizens' rights to criticize the government.

Most of the cases dealing with the Free Speech Clause that have reached the Supreme Court involve state laws. The Supreme Court first incorporated the Free Speech Clause to apply to the states in *Gitlow v. New York* (1925). In this case, the Court upheld the conviction of Benjamin Gitlow under New York's Criminal Anarchy Law on the grounds that Gitlow advocated the overthrow of the government.

However, two justices dissented from the *Gitlow* decision, as Gitlow's socialist manifesto was unlikely to result in any violent action against the government.

PROTECTIONS OF FREEDOM OF SPEECH

Since incorporating the Free Speech Clause, the Supreme Court has handed down several decisions protecting broad categories of speech, including on-campus and hate speech.

Speech on Campus

The Supreme Court has upheld the rights of students to express themselves freely on campus as long as the speech does not create a substantial disruption to the school environment. In *Tinker v. Des Moines* (1969), the Court ruled in favor of students who wore black armbands to school to protest the Vietnam War. The school's suspension of the students was overturned, as school officials were unable to demonstrate that the students' free speech disrupted academic instruction.

Symbolic Speech

The Supreme Court has given Americans generous leeway when it comes to expressing themselves symbolically, even to the point of desecrating national symbols. In *Texas v. Johnson* (1989), a divided Court overturned the conviction of Gregory Johnson, who had been arrested for burning an American flag. The *Texas v. Johnson* case put justices in the uncomfortable position of choosing between the

American flag and the First Amendment. "Sometimes we must make decisions we do not like," wrote Justice Anthony Kennedy.

Hate Speech

The United States is one of only a few developed countries that doesn't criminalize hate speech. Although civil rights legislation prohibits discrimination by employers and educational institutions based on race, religion, sexual orientation, and gender identity, the First Amendment protects hate speech by individuals and groups acting in private capacities. In *Snyder v. Phelps* (2011), the Supreme Court ruled in favor of Fred Phelps, a pastor who repeatedly used the funerals of deceased Iraq War veterans as a platform for making offensive and homophobic remarks. In the opinion of a nearly unanimous Court, Phelps's right to free speech outweighed the interests of veterans' mourning families.

LIMITATIONS ON FREEDOM OF SPEECH

Although the First Amendment generously protects nearly every form of politically oriented and opinionated speech, the Supreme Court has ruled that there are a few limits to what Americans can say.

Seditious Speech

Seditious speech is when someone's speech could reasonably result in the overthrow of the government or contribute to its inability to conduct its necessary functions during wartime. During World War I, Congress passed the Espionage and Sedition Acts, which forbade Americans from a host of activities that were deemed to undermine the war effort, including desecrating the US flag, displaying the flag of an enemy nation, or engaging in speech that would undermine military recruitment or wartime production.

"Clear and Present Danger"

After World War I, the Supreme Court sought to place limits on the government's ability to restrict free speech during wartime while at the same time allowing prosecutions when seditious speech threatened to stop the government from performing its core functions. In *Schenck v. United States* (1919), the Court upheld the conviction of Charles Schenck, who had actively encouraged young men to break the law by resisting the draft. Justice Oliver Wendell Holmes Jr. wrote the Court's unanimous opinion, which outlined the limitations of free speech.

> The most stringent protection of free speech would not protect a man in falsely shouting fire in a theatre and causing a panic.… The question…is whether the words used are used in such circumstances and are of such a nature as to create a clear and present danger that they will bring about the substantive evils that Congress has a right to prevent.
>
> —*Schenck v. United States* (1919)

The "clear and present danger" test established a standard for criminalizing seditious speech that the Court would rely on for several decades.

"Imminent Lawless Action"

In *Brandenburg v. Ohio* (1969), the Supreme Court rejected the "clear and present danger" test for the more lenient "imminent lawless action" test when it ruled in favor of Clarence Brandenburg, a Ku Klux Klan member in Ohio. Brandenburg had made several hateful statements advocating the forced expulsion of Black people and Jewish people from the United States. The Court ruled that an American cannot be punished for abstract hateful statements threatening violence against the government or minority groups unless government authorities could demonstrate that the statements were likely to result in "imminent lawless action."

Speech on Campus

Although students enjoy the right to express their political and religious views at school (as long as they are not disruptive), schools are allowed to discipline students for indecent speech. In *Bethel School District v. Fraser* (1986), the Court upheld the suspension of a student who gave a speech at a school assembly that was filled with sexually suggestive innuendo.

Slander and Defamation

The First Amendment prohibits slander, a form of defamation in which a person makes oral statements about another person or business entity that are both untrue and damaging. In order to be considered slander, a statement must be false and must also cause economic or reputational damage to the victim. Furthermore, it must be proven that the person engaging in slander knew that what they were saying was untrue.

FREEDOM OF THE PRESS

To Print or Not to Print?

The First Amendment prohibits Congress from making any law "abridging the freedom...of the press." In doing so, the Constitution protects the freedom of the published word just as it protects the freedom of the spoken word. The freedom of the press protects newspapers, magazines, television broadcasts, websites, art, and literature from arbitrary censorship by the government. However, just as some forms of speech lie beyond the protection of the First Amendment, libelous and obscene publications may be subject to legal action.

THE SEDITION ACT OF 1798

In 1798, Congress tested the First Amendment's guarantees of freedom of the press. Amid escalating tensions with France, Congress passed the Sedition Act, prohibiting the publication of false and malicious statements about government officials. The Sedition Act was a political tool devised by the Federalist Party, which controlled the presidency and Congress, to prosecute newspaper publishers who supported Thomas Jefferson's Republican Party. Both Jefferson (the author of the Declaration of Independence) and James Madison (the father of the Constitution) wrote resolutions protesting the unconstitutional and politically motivated legislation. Jefferson was elected president in 1800, and the Sedition Act expired the following year, so it became a moot point. Congress would not pass another sedition act until World War I.

LIBEL

Just as freedom of speech is not inclusive of the right to slander, freedom of the press is not inclusive of libel. Publishers of newspapers, magazines, and books are responsible for the content they publish—they can be held liable if they knowingly publish false information with malicious intent. However, the standard for seeking damages for libel is high; a plaintiff seeking damages must prove that the publisher knowingly printed something that was both malicious and untrue.

Libel and Liability

When discussing freedom of the press, it is easy to confuse the related concepts of libel and liability. Libel describes the publication of material that is false, scandalous, and malicious. Liability involves legal responsibility for damages in a civil lawsuit (the equivalent of a guilty verdict). A publisher of libelous content risks being held liable for damages suffered by the victim(s).

The most important Supreme Court case involving journalistic libel is *New York Times v. Sullivan* (1964). During the civil rights movement, *The New York Times* published an advertisement that was critical of the Montgomery Police Department's handling of peaceful protests led by Dr. Martin Luther King Jr. The advertisement exaggerated the number of times that King had been arrested in Montgomery and referenced "truckloads of police," sensationalizing the degree to which Montgomery police intimidated the protesters. The Montgomery police commissioner sued the *Times* for libel based on the inaccuracies in the article. In a unanimous decision, the Court ruled in favor of the *Times*, finding the inaccuracies to be honest mistakes rather than libelous attacks published with malicious intent. The ruling established the "actual malice standard" for proving libel.

SATIRE

The First Amendment protects the rights of publishers to publish false and scandalous content if the content is intended to be satirical. In 1983, *Hustler* magazine, known for its pornographic content and salacious humor, published a parody of then-popular Campari liqueur advertisements in which conservative televangelist Jerry Falwell was depicted talking about his "first time." Falwell sued for defamation and emotional distress. A jury ruled against Falwell's libel claim but awarded him $150,000 in damages for emotional distress on the grounds that *Hustler* magazine had published the satirical piece to purposefully inflict emotional distress.

In the appeal of that case, the Supreme Court ruled unanimously in *Hustler Magazine v. Falwell* (1988) that *Hustler* magazine could not be held liable for emotional distress. Satirical humor at the expense of public figures is protected by the First Amendment even when it is malicious. Holding *Hustler* liable would have endangered freedom of the press by denying Americans the right to use off-color humor to criticize public figures.

OBSCENITY

The First Amendment also protects the production of literature and art that people may find offensive. However, these protections do not extend to the publication of obscene materials that depict lewd acts for their own sake and are devoid of literary or artistic value. Both Congress and state legislatures have reserved the right to regulate obscene expression. In 1873, Congress passed the Comstock laws, which banned the circulation of "obscene literature" through the postal service. The Comstock laws faced little opposition in the nineteenth century but would encounter several challenges in the next century as the idea of "obscenity" changed over time.

The Supreme Court has been faced with the unenviable task of defining the line between valid artistic expression and obscenity. In *Memoirs v. Massachusetts* (1966), the Court defined obscene materials as having no redeeming social value—a standard so low that it was difficult to classify anything as obscene. The Court clarified this when a California restaurant owner complained about receiving an unsolicited pornographic catalog from Marvin Miller, a pornography distributor. In *Miller v. California* (1973), the Court rejected Miller's claim that the materials in his catalog were not obscene and considered the catalog's contents as a whole rather than evaluating whether the catalog had even an ounce of artistic value. The Court's formula for defining obscenity, the Miller test, instructed juries to consider the following:

1. Would the average person applying "contemporary community standards" find the work to appeal to "prurient interests"?
2. Does the work depict or describe sexual conduct in an offensive way as defined by state law?
3. Does the entirety of the work lack "serious literary, artistic, political, or scientific value"?

While the Miller test does not offer a precise definition of obscenity, it does allow juries some flexibility in defining obscenity to allow for regional differences and changing times.

PRIOR RESTRAINT

The Supreme Court has largely frowned upon the practice of prior restraint. This is when government officials prohibit the publication of material dangerous to government interests. However, there are some cases in which prior restraint is acceptable to protect national security, such as publishing classified information about troop deployments during wartime. In *New York Times v. United States* (1971), the Court rejected the Nixon administration's use of prior restraint to keep the *Times* from publishing the *Pentagon Papers*, which contained thousands of pages of government documents leaked by Daniel Ellsberg, a government contractor. The Nixon administration claimed that the documents should remain secret based on executive privilege; however, the Court's majority believed that the Nixon administration failed to demonstrate that the publication of the documents presented a vital risk to national security.

The Court's decision in *New York Times v. United States* presented government officials with a high bar for inhibiting the freedom of the press. The publication of the *Pentagon Papers* caused great embarrassment to government officials who had lied to the American people about US conduct during the Vietnam War. While the government has a right to protect national security, it does not have a right to protect government officials from embarrassment.

FREEDOM OF ASSEMBLY AND PETITION

Constitutional Protections of Collective Speech

In addition to protecting the rights of Americans to express themselves individually, the Constitution protects the rights of groups to express themselves collectively through peaceful assemblies and petitions to the government. The First Amendment protects the exercise of the right to protest and the expression of grievances against the government without fear of arrest or prosecution.

> Congress shall make no law respecting...the right of the people peaceably to assemble, and to petition the Government for a redress of grievances.
>
> —Amendment I to the Constitution

THE RIGHT TO ASSEMBLE

The right to peaceful assembly obligates both the federal and state governments to allow Americans to engage in public demonstrations and protests, as long as the protests are orderly and nonviolent. It also protects the freedom of association, such as joining political organizations and labor unions. In *De Jonge v. Oregon* (1937), the Supreme Court incorporated the right to assemble as binding on the states. In *Edwards v. South Carolina* (1963), the Court ruled that South Carolina officials violated the rights of civil rights protesters by arresting them after they defied orders to disperse their peaceful protest in front of the state capitol.

Limitations on the Right to Assemble

The right of assembly is bound by similar limitations as the right to free speech. Although the Supreme Court has upheld the right to assemblies that advocate for the overthrow of the US government in the abstract (such as organizations associated with communism), it does not protect assemblies that are organized with concrete plans to do so.

No Right to Riot

In order to be protected by the First Amendment, protests must be orderly and peaceful. If protesters become riotous, government officials may intervene with police powers.

Armed Demonstrations

The right to carry weapons at a protest is not protected by the First Amendment. Protesters must follow state and federal weapons laws. In 2020, gun rights advocates in Virginia rallied at the state capitol, drawing over twenty thousand participants, several of whom openly carried firearms during the protest. Although the protesters were peaceful and acted in accordance with state laws permitting the open carry of firearms, the governor acted within his authority by calling additional police to Richmond on the day of the event.

Protest Permits

In *Shuttlesworth v. Birmingham* (1969), the Supreme Court struck down a city ordinance in Birmingham, Alabama, requiring civil rights organizations to apply for a permit before protesting. Although the *Shuttlesworth* decision does not stop city governments from requiring permits to protest, the permit process must be objective, have a clear public safety purpose, and not be aimed at suppressing the right to protest.

THE RIGHT TO PETITION

The right to petition won't be found on many people's "top ten" lists of constitutional rights today, but the Founding Fathers had important reasons for including it in the First Amendment. In authoritarian states, simply submitting a petition can be considered an act of treason against the government. The right to petition, even if invoked infrequently, protects Americans from being considered disloyal for expressing disagreements with government policy.

English Precedents

The right to petition has firm roots in the English constitutional tradition. The Magna Carta acknowledged the right of representative assemblies to petition the king. In 1628, Parliament passed the Petition of Right, which denounced the corrupt and unconstitutional practices of government officials during the reign of Charles I (while still pledging personal loyalty to the king). Although Charles received the Petition of Right, he dissolved Parliament the following year. Two revolutions against the monarchy—one the result of a bloody civil war and the other comparatively bloodless—followed in the ensuing decades, resulting in the right to petition being included in the English Bill of Rights in 1689.

The American Revolution

In the years leading up to the American Revolution, American colonists became frustrated with King George III, who tended to either ignore their petitions or receive them unfavorably. In 1775, he rejected the Olive Branch Petition, in which the Second Continental Congress declared its loyalty to him and requested his intervention in its dispute with Parliament.

The Gag Rule

Although Americans have a right to petition the government without fear of facing legal reprisals, the Constitution does not obligate government officials to favorably receive petitions. In the 1830s, abolitionist societies began flooding Congress with petitions against slavery, which citizens in the North saw as a violation of their natural rights. Southern congressmen viewed these petitions as threats to the economic and social foundations of their society. Aided by Northern congressmen who saw the petitions as a threat to sectional harmony, they succeeded in getting the House of Representatives to pass a "gag rule" on the consideration of antislavery petitions in the 1830s. Although it was eventually repealed, the gag rule illustrated that the government could ignore petitions without violating the First Amendment's right to petition the government.

Petitions in Contemporary America

There have been efforts to revitalize the right to petition in the digital age, but they have largely fallen flat. In 2011, the White House created a page on its website to receive petitions from Americans, promising to respond to those that received enough signatures. However, one of the most popular petitions called for the White House to allow Republican-leaning states to secede from the Union following President Barack Obama's reelection. Another called for the federal government to construct a "Death Star" battle station in the style of the Star Wars movies. The comedic and unserious nature of many of the most popular petitions led the White House to shut down the page in 2021. Few Americans are likely to miss it.

THE RIGHT TO BEAR ARMS

The Constitution's Most Controversial Right

The United States is the only nation that has more guns than people. According to the 2017 Small Arms Survey, there are over 120 guns in America for every 100 residents. However, according to a 2023 survey from Gallup, less than half of Americans reported that they own a firearm. The United States is alone among developed nations in allowing the private ownership of firearms without a permit. The right to private ownership of firearms is both a cherished right of Americans and a concern due to gun-related violence and mass shootings. The prevalence of gun ownership in America is the product of the intersection between American sporting culture and the constitutional protections provided by the Second Amendment.

THE SECOND AMENDMENT

A well regulated Militia, being necessary to the security of a free State, the right of the people to keep and bear Arms, shall not be infringed.
—Amendment II to the Constitution

INTERPRETING THE SECOND AMENDMENT

During the twentieth century, the Supreme Court incorporated most of the Bill of Rights onto the states while remaining silent about the

Second Amendment. No case prior to 2008 prompted the Supreme Court to rule definitively on whether the Second Amendment protects an individual's right to keep and bear arms. This created an atmosphere of uncertainty that sparked fierce debate. Advocates of gun rights stressed the closing clause ("shall not be infringed") to argue against government regulation of firearms. Advocates of gun control, however, focused on the opening clause, which indicates a connection between the right to bear arms and service in a state militia.

"A Well Regulated Militia"

Today, regulation is understood almost exclusively in terms of the government's rulemaking powers. However, in the context of the eighteenth century, regulation was used more often to describe procedures for military drills. The phrase "A well regulated militia" should be understood to describe a militia that was well disciplined and combat-ready.

An Individual Right

In 2008, the Supreme Court settled the debate over the Second Amendment in *District of Columbia v. Heller* with a 5–4 ruling. The Court ruled that the Second Amendment protects an individual's right to own a firearm for self-defense regardless of involvement with a state militia. The *Heller* decision struck down the District of Columbia's ban on private ownership of handguns.

INCORPORATION OF THE SECOND AMENDMENT

A few years after the *Heller* decision, the Supreme Court began incorporating the Second Amendment to apply to state governments on the basis of the Fourteenth Amendment's Due Process Clause. This clause prohibits states from depriving citizens of life, liberty, or property without due process of law.

The Right to Keep Arms

In *McDonald v. Chicago* (2010), the Court struck down Chicago's city ordinances, which made it extremely difficult for someone to register a firearm. According to the ruling, Chicago had deprived Otis McDonald, a law-abiding citizen, of his right to keep a handgun in his home for self-defense without due process of law.

The Right to Bear Arms

In 2023, the Supreme Court incorporated the right to carry a firearm outside the home, striking down a New York law that required applicants for concealed carry permits to show "proper cause" for carrying a pistol for protection. Although states have the authority to establish requirements for the issuing of concealed carry permits, such as completing a training course and having a clean criminal record, states cannot require people to demonstrate a special need to exercise a constitutional right.

LIMITATIONS ON SECOND AMENDMENT RIGHTS

The Supreme Court has handed down several decisions supporting Second Amendment rights in the abstract; however, the government does have the power to regulate the ownership and use of firearms.

Convicted Felons

The Supreme Court has not struck down any state or federal laws that bar convicted felons (and those convicted of violent misdemeanors) from owning firearms. Unlike Otis McDonald, convicted criminals no longer have the right to bear arms after receiving due process (a fair trial, legal counsel, etc.). However, the Supreme Court has yet to decide whether nonviolent felons, such as those convicted of tax evasion, must forfeit their Second Amendment rights.

The Right to Carry

The Supreme Court allows the states to regulate the open carrying of firearms in public places. For example, states have the authority to place restrictions on certain locations where firearms can be carried, typically schools, courthouses, and hospitals. During the civil rights movement, some states enacted laws against open carry in response to peaceful, but armed, demonstrations by members of the Black Panther Party. In 1967, California governor Ronald Reagan signed the Mulford Act, which prohibited people from carrying loaded weapons in public. Reagan, a conservative, stated that he saw "no reason why on the street today a citizen should be carrying loaded weapons." Gun control legislation enjoyed bipartisan support until the National Rifle Association, a powerful lobbying organization representing gun owners, mobilized against the Brady Handgun Violence Prevention Act, which passed Congress in 1993.

The debate over the Brady Act shifted the issue of gun regulation from one of broad bipartisan consensus to one of increasing partisan polarization. While the Supreme Court has recently declared individual ownership of firearms to be a right protected by the Second Amendment and incorporated into the states, it has largely left the determination of the fine print to the elected branches of government.

PUBLIC OPINION ON THE SECOND AMENDMENT

Although there is a broad consensus supporting gun ownership as an individual right, a majority of Americans support stricter government regulation of gun ownership. Gallup polls in 2023 show that 56 percent of Americans support stricter government regulations of gun sales, but only 27 percent of Americans support an outright ban on private handgun ownership. Public opinion on gun ownership largely aligns with the Supreme Court's recent decisions to protect the right of individual gun ownership while allowing for regulations by federal and state governments.

THE RIGHT TO DUE PROCESS

Dotting I's and Crossing T's

The Bill of Rights highlights the right to due process in matters of criminal law. Due process creates a set procedure the government can use to proceed against criminal suspects. This protects those accused of a crime from arbitrary or malicious actions by government officials. Most of the Constitution's guarantees for criminal due process are found in the Fourth Amendment, which protects Americans from unreasonable searches and seizures, and the Fifth Amendment, which ensures that no American will have to stand trial without evidence or be compelled to present evidence against themselves.

THE FOURTH AMENDMENT

The Fourth Amendment was added to the Constitution so that federal officials could not search an American's personal property without both probable cause and a warrant clearly describing the items sought by government officials.

> The right of the people to be secure in their persons, houses, papers, and effects, against unreasonable searches and seizures, shall not be violated, and no Warrants shall issue, but upon probable cause...particularly describing the place to be searched, and the persons or things to be seized.
>
> —Amendment IV to the Constitution

English Precedents

The Fourth Amendment is heavily influenced by the English legal tradition. "The house of every one is to him as his castle and fortress," wrote Sir Edward Coke, a prominent legal scholar of the Elizabethan era. Coke's castle doctrine asserts that government officials do not have the right to enter a private home without the owner's permission or probable cause to believe that evidence of criminal activity is to be found there.

Protection Against General Warrants

In the thirteen colonies, colonists did not have the same rights as English citizens. Colonial officials often used general warrants to search homes, which gave government officials the power to search the home for any evidence of criminal activity. During the American Revolution, the Founding Fathers took advantage of the opportunity to ban general warrants. George Mason's Virginia Declaration of Rights prohibited the use of general warrants, barring government officials from seizing any person or item not specifically named in the warrant. In Massachusetts, John Adams added a clarification that searches must be "reasonable," meaning that the government had demonstrated probable cause for the search. The Fourth Amendment was constructed using this language, which had already been adopted by many of the states.

The Exclusionary Rule

The Fourth Amendment is the basis for the exclusionary rule, which prohibits government officials from using evidence against a criminal defendant that was not acquired by the due process outlined by the Fourth Amendment. The Supreme Court incorporated the exclusionary rule to the states in *Mapp v. Ohio* (1961) when it overturned the conviction of Dollree Mapp, who was prosecuted for the possession of pornography that was obtained in a warrantless search.

THE FIFTH AMENDMENT

The Fifth Amendment enshrines due process by protecting Americans from being prosecuted without sufficient evidence, tried twice for the same crime, and compelled to self-incriminate by providing evidence against themselves.

> No person shall be held to answer for a capital, or otherwise infamous crime, unless on a presentment or indictment of a Grand Jury...nor shall any person be subject for the same offence to be twice put in jeopardy of life or limb; nor shall be compelled in any criminal case to be a witness against himself, nor be deprived of life, liberty, or property, without due process of law.
>
> —Amendment V to the Constitution

A Grand Jury

Unlike a trial jury, which determines a defendant's guilt, a grand jury is convened to decide whether government prosecutors have enough evidence to formally charge a defendant with a crime. This protects Americans from frivolous and malicious prosecution. Curiously, the grand jury requirement of the Fifth Amendment remains one of the few provisions of the Bill of Rights that has not been incorporated onto the states. Although most states use grand juries, the federal nature of the Constitution enables the states to use other means besides a grand jury to protect defendants from malicious prosecution.

The Right to Remain Silent

Because of the Fifth Amendment, Americans don't have to provide evidence against themselves during police interrogation or at trial. The American legal system is based on the idea that the government has the burden of proof, and a defendant's guilt is decided exclusively based on the strength of the government's case. If a defendant (or a witness) is asked a question that, if answered honestly, would implicate them in a criminal act, they have the right to "plead the Fifth" in lieu of answering the question.

The Right to Know One's Rights

Americans not only have the right to remain silent; they also have the right to be informed of this right. In *Miranda v. Arizona* (1966), the Supreme Court overturned a guilty verdict against Ernesto Miranda, who had freely confessed to the crimes of kidnapping and rape. While Miranda's confession was not in any way coerced by police, the police never informed him that he had a right to remain silent.

Double Jeopardy

The Constitution protects Americans from "double jeopardy," which involves being tried twice for the same crime. After a "not guilty" verdict, there is nothing the government can do even if the defendant later confesses to committing the crime. Stopping short of an outright confession, O.J. Simpson signed a book deal several years after his murder trial to publish *If I Did It*, which presented a hypothetical scenario of how he may have gone about murdering Nicole Brown Simpson and Ron Goldman. Since he had already received a "not guilty" verdict, nothing in this book could be used against him in a retrial.

The Double Jeopardy Clause does not always apply in the case of a mistrial in which standard due process procedures were not followed. After Ernesto Miranda's conviction was overturned by the Supreme Court, the state of Arizona retried him for the same offense, resulting in a guilty verdict due to witness testimony.

THE RIGHT TO A FAIR TRIAL

Setting the Rules for Real Life's Legal Dramas

The moment when a suspect, having been backed into a corner during a police interrogation, asks for their attorney is very common in legal dramas. Such a request effectively levels the playing field when a person accused of a crime finds themselves facing the entire weight of the legal system alone. Without legal counsel from an attorney, a criminal defendant is often outmatched. An attorney acts as a shield for their client, protecting them from mistakes they might make due to ignorance of trial procedure. In addition, attorneys assist their clients throughout the trial process, using their experience speaking before juries, gathering evidence, and questioning witnesses to offer the maximum advantage to their clients.

THE SIXTH AMENDMENT

The Sixth Amendment to the Constitution guarantees that criminal defendants have the following rights: to have a trial that is both speedy and public, to have their case decided by a jury, to call and question witnesses, and to have an attorney to assist them throughout the entire process.

In all criminal prosecutions, the accused shall enjoy the right to a speedy and public trial, by an impartial jury of the State and district wherein the crime shall have been committed, which district shall have been previously ascertained by law, and to be informed of the nature and cause of the accusation; to be confronted with the witnesses against him; to have compulsory process for obtaining witnesses in his favor, and to have the Assistance of Counsel for his defence.

—Amendment VI to the Constitution

The Right to a Speedy Trial

The Constitution grants all Americans the right to a speedy trial, meaning that a defendant will have their case brought to trial without unreasonable delays. Given the wide variety of criminal cases involving both major and minor offenses, there is no hard-and-fast timetable that defines a speedy trial. For example, federal prosecutors would need more time to prepare to prosecute a high-profile money-laundering case than for a case of someone arrested for simple possession of illegal drugs on federal property. That said, an individual case against a defendant can be dismissed due to an unreasonable delay in the trial.

The Right to a Public Trial

Generally, the Constitution requires that trials be convened in public because of the presumption that what happens in plain sight is less likely to be corrupt. The Founding Fathers had historical memories of the Star Chamber, a special English court in which defendants were placed on trial in private proceedings. While historians debate the extent to which the Star Chamber's proceedings were *actually* corrupt, proponents of the Bill of Rights didn't want to see such a court in the United States.

The right to a public trial is not absolute. There are limited cases in which a trial can be convened privately, such as those in which a public trial would involve the release of classified information that is deemed vital for national security. A defendant can also request a private trial when a public trial could endanger their right to a fair trial.

An Impartial Jury

A trial by jury is one of the most well-known rights protected by the Bill of Rights. While the Supreme Court has incorporated the right to a jury trial onto the states and requires states to ensure a jury's impartiality, state courts are not bound by the Sixth Amendment's Vicinage Clause, which requires the jury to be chosen from the state and district in which the alleged crime was committed.

Confronting and Calling Witnesses

The Sixth Amendment guarantees a defendant's right to confront and question witnesses who appear against them in front of a jury. This allows defense attorneys to expose any inconsistencies in the testimonies of prosecution witnesses as well as to question the credibility and character of these witnesses. Additionally, defendants may issue subpoenas to witnesses to appear in their defense, requiring witnesses to appear in court if they have testimony that might shed reasonable doubt upon the defendant's guilt.

The Right to Counsel

The Sixth Amendment guarantees that all criminal defendants have access to legal counsel. Although this right was initially only applicable to federal courts, the Supreme Court incorporated the right to counsel for all criminal defendants onto the states in *Gideon v. Wainwright* (1963). The Court agreed to hear the case of Clarence Gideon, who had been found guilty of breaking into a pool hall and stealing change from a cigarette machine. Gideon, who could not afford an attorney, was refused legal counsel because, at the time,

Florida law only provided an attorney to defendants who were charged with capital offenses (felony offenses for which the death penalty was a possible punishment). While in jail, Gideon petitioned the Court with a handwritten note that he wrote in prison after reading books about the legal system in the prison library. After the Supreme Court's unanimous decision in his favor, Gideon's case was retried, resulting in a verdict of "not guilty."

Public Defenders

The Sixth Amendment requires both the federal and state governments to commission public defenders, lawyers whose sole responsibility is to provide legal defense to clients who lack the financial means to hire an attorney. Public defenders work to make sure that criminal defendants have the right to a fair trial regardless of whether they can afford legal counsel.

When ratified, the Sixth Amendment's guarantee of a right to an attorney was ahead of its time, as no such right existed at that time in the British system. It was believed that innocent defendants did not require counsel, as all such a defendant had to do was tell the truth.

CRUEL AND UNUSUAL PUNISHMENTS

Protecting the Rights of Those Detained and Condemned

In medieval England, those convicted of treason were often sentenced to be hanged, drawn, and quartered. This painful punishment involved a convicted person being dragged behind a horse to the place of their execution where they were hanged until near death before being disemboweled, dismembered, and beheaded. Thanks to the Eighth Amendment, no American has ever faced punishment like this (no matter how serious their criminal offense).

THE EIGHTH AMENDMENT

Excessive bail shall not be required, nor excessive fines imposed, nor cruel and unusual punishments inflicted.

—Amendment VIII to the Constitution

The Eighth Amendment to the Constitution was designed to ensure that punishments fit the crime and that pretrial defendants would not rot in jail while awaiting trial. This amendment has roots in both the English legal tradition and the philosophical ideas from the Enlightenment.

English Traditions

England, like most European nations, had a history of inflicting painful, torturous punishments on convicted criminals. However, the Glorious Revolution of 1688–1689 presented an occasion for Parliament and the newly coronated joint monarchs William and Mary to agree to place limits on the state's ability to inflict painful punishments. The English Bill of Rights stated that "excessive bail ought not to be required, nor excessive fines imposed, nor cruel and unusual punishment inflicted."

Enlightenment Influence

Enlightenment philosophers of the eighteenth century questioned the use of torture in criminal proceedings and as a punishment. Their writings reflected a growing consensus that guilt should be based only on the evidence presented and that those found guilty deserved a humane punishment. Cesare Beccaria, an Italian lawyer and philosopher, published *On Crimes and Punishments* in 1764, in which he criticized the death penalty on the basis that life, being a natural right, cannot be taken away from an individual by the state.

Excessive Bails

The Eighth Amendment protects Americans from receiving excessive bails, meaning that a judge cannot impose a bail larger than what is deemed to be required to ensure that a criminal defendant will appear in court. Although the Eighth Amendment prohibits judges from setting excessive bails, it does not guarantee bail to someone who may flee or has been accused of a serious violent crime, justifying a defendant's placement in jail for public safety until the trial.

The prohibition on excessive bails complements the Constitution's prohibition on the suspension of the rights of habeas corpus. The right of habeas corpus (literally, "you shall have the body") generally prohibits government officials from holding individuals for long periods of time without formally charging them with a crime. Article I, Section 9 of the Constitution states: "The Privilege of the Writ of Habeas Corpus shall not be suspended, unless when in Cases of Rebellion or Invasion the public Safety may require it." There are special circumstances that allow government officials to hold people for extended times without charge, as Abraham Lincoln did with suspected secessionists in Maryland in 1861, whose activities threatened to place the federal capital between two seceded states.

What Is Bail?

Bail is an amount of money assessed by a court in order to guarantee that a defendant will reappear in court for their trial. If a defendant who has paid bail (either personally or through posting a bail bond) shows up at their trial, they receive the money back. Defendants who do not appear in court for their trial forfeit bail in addition to becoming fugitives from justice.

Excessive Fines

The Excessive Fines Clause of the Eighth Amendment protects Americans from being fined in ways that are so excessive as to constitute the loss of property without due process. This clause was incorporated to apply to the states under the Due Process Clause of the Fourteenth Amendment.

Punitive damages awarded to plaintiffs in civil lawsuits are not expressly covered under the Eighth Amendment, which governs criminal procedures, but they can be declared excessive based on the Fourteenth Amendment's Due Process Clause.

Cruel and Unusual

A precise definition of "cruel and unusual" may be evasive, but the term generally describes punishments that are unnecessarily painful, undermine human dignity, are of unnecessary severity, or are administered arbitrarily without any clear consistency.

Capital Punishment

Although the Supreme Court has never ruled capital punishment to be cruel and unusual in and of itself, the Court once ordered a moratorium (pause) on capital punishment in *Furman v. Georgia* (1972) on the basis that capital punishment was being applied arbitrarily with clear evidence of racial biases. The Court ended the moratorium four years later after states had demonstrated sufficient reforms in their legal systems.

With the passage of a Virginia law in 2021 ending capital punishment in the state, twenty-three states have abolished the death penalty. Although a narrow majority of the states still sanction the use of capital punishment, executions are becoming increasingly rare.

States have some flexibility in determining their execution methods, as long as the approved methods in each state do not violate the Eighth Amendment's prohibition on cruel and unusual punishment. During the twentieth century, the electric chair was the most common method of execution. In the twenty-first century, lethal injection is currently the most common method, with some states resorting to alternate methods because of an increasing scarcity of the drugs required to administer this form of execution. Five states (Idaho, Mississippi, Oklahoma, South Carolina, and Utah) currently sanction the use of firing squads as a faster and more humane alternative to lethal injection.

Recent Developments

The discussion of the death penalty is ongoing, as fewer Americans support the practice compared to a generation ago. A 2023 Gallup poll revealed that a narrow majority of 53 percent of Americans continue to support the death penalty (compared to 80 percent in 1991), while only 47 percent believe that it is administered fairly. Since punishments that are not supported by the public are likely to be considered cruel and unusual, the future of the death penalty is uncertain.

THE RIGHT TO PRIVACY

A Right Not Stated but Strongly Implied

Americans take their privacy seriously. One seldom opens a website for the first time without being asked to validate privacy settings. Laws have been passed to protect Americans from a number of invasions of their privacy, from identity theft to stalking. However, no part of the Constitution directly mentions privacy as a right of the people. So, what is the extent to which a right to privacy exists under the Constitution? While a number of Supreme Court decisions have reinforced the idea of a constitutional right to privacy, other decisions have just as clearly shown that this right is subject to limitations.

PRIVACY AND THE CONSTITUTION

Advocates of a constitutional right to privacy base their belief on the presence of several explicit guarantees in the Bill of Rights. Taken together, these rights imply that privacy was presumed by the framers to the point that it did not need to be specifically mentioned.

- **First Amendment:** This amendment's guarantees of freedom of religion and speech protect the private thoughts that are necessary to form religious and political opinions. Plus, the freedom of assembly protects private meetings and associations.
- **Third Amendment:** This amendment, which prohibits the government from quartering soldiers in private homes during peacetime, presumes that Americans have a right not to be disturbed in their homes unless there is an urgent need.

- **Fourth Amendment:** This amendment protects the right of the people "to be secure in their persons, houses, papers, and effects, against unreasonable searches and seizures." This is the Constitution's strongest case for a right to privacy, designating a person's house and property as a private sphere protected from government interference unless a warrant is issued.
- **Fifth Amendment:** This amendment's protections against self-incrimination implies a right to privacy by acknowledging an individual's right to keep potentially incriminating information private.
- **Ninth Amendment:** This amendment states: "The enumeration in the Constitution, of certain rights, shall not be construed to deny or disparage others retained by the people." In other words, the rights protected by the first eight amendments to the Constitution are not intended to be an exhaustive list. Additionally, the federal government should never be presumed to have additional powers beyond what is in the Constitution.
- **Fourteenth Amendment:** The Supreme Court holds that the Due Process Clause of this amendment protects Americans from government actions that frivolously undermine their privacy without a legitimate public interest to justify the government action.

PRIVACY AND THE COURTS

The Supreme Court has considered several cases regarding the constitutional right to privacy, with its decisions evolving based on the ideological composition of the Court at any given time. Most of the recent decisions have focused on reproductive privacy.

Griswold v. Connecticut

In *Griswold v. Connecticut* (1965), the Court struck down a Connecticut law that banned the use of birth control. The Court's 7-2 decision reflected the majority's belief that a married couple's use of birth control was constitutionally protected by the right to marital privacy, which gives married couples the right to make intimate decisions without government interference. The *Griswold* decision was based on the "penumbra" of guarantees of privacy found in the Bill of Rights.

Roe v. Wade

In *Roe v. Wade* (1973), the Supreme Court struck down a Texas law that criminalized abortion as a medical procedure unless it was performed to save the life of the mother. The Court based its ruling on the Due Process Clause of the Fourteenth Amendment. Although the *Roe* decision prohibited states from banning abortion procedures outright, it did allow states to regulate late-term abortions in order to protect potential life once it has reached the age of viability (twenty weeks).

Planned Parenthood v. Casey

In the decades following *Roe v. Wade*, some states tested the waters to find out how far they could go in regulating abortion. Following the presidencies of Ronald Reagan and George H. W. Bush, conservatives hoped that the Supreme Court's recently confirmed justices would overturn *Roe*. In *Planned Parenthood v. Casey* (1992), the Court upheld Roe as precedent but also upheld Pennsylvania laws that mandated parental consent for minors seeking to have abortions, a twenty-four-hour waiting period for abortions, and "informed consent" (doctors must provide details of the procedure to those seeking abortions). However, the Court struck down a law requiring married women to have the consent of their husbands prior to the procedure.

Dobbs v. Jackson Women's Health Organization

In *Dobbs v. Jackson Women's Health Organization* (2022), the Supreme Court overturned both *Roe* and *Casey* in a 5–4 decision, holding that abortion is not a right protected by the Constitution. The *Dobbs* decision resulted in each state making its own regulations regarding abortion (in the absence of congressional legislation). That said, the majority opinion in *Dobbs* upheld the general idea of a constitutional right to privacy, while placing abortion outside of the sphere of the protection of the right to privacy.

CRITICISMS OF A CONSTITUTIONAL RIGHT TO PRIVACY

Although the idea of a constitutional right to privacy has broad support among Americans, legal scholars are not unanimous concerning its existence. In his dissenting opinion in the *Griswold* decision, Justice Hugo Black expressed concern that reading the Fourth Amendment as a protection of a right to privacy could result in substituting the Fourth Amendment's specific protections and guarantees with something more ambiguous. More recently, Justice Clarence Thomas wrote in an opinion concurring with the *Dobbs* decision that the Court should revisit *Griswold* and the idea of a constitutional right to privacy. The bounds of this right are still being determined today.

THE RIGHTS OF THE STATES

Defining the Great Line Between Federal and State
Power

The Constitution creates a federal system of government whereby the federal and state governments each have sovereignty within their distinct spheres. While the Constitution operates under the authority of "We the People," the states are important entities within the governing arrangement created by the Constitution. The Articles of Confederation clearly assert the rights of the states by declaring: "Each state retains its sovereignty, freedom and independence, and every Power...which is not by this confederation expressly delegated to the United States, in Congress assembled." During the ratification debates, Antifederalists objected that this language wasn't replicated in the original Constitution. As a compromise, the Tenth Amendment was included in the Bill of Rights to explicitly protect the rights of the states.

THE TENTH AMENDMENT

The Tenth Amendment to the Constitution was written to clarify that the states retain any powers they had not agreed to give to the federal government. It reads:

> The powers not delegated to the United States by the Constitution, nor prohibited by it to the States, are reserved to the States respectively, or to the people.
>
> —Amendment X to the Constitution

When introducing the Tenth Amendment to Congress, James Madison claimed that the amendment's spirit was already present in the original Constitution's delegation of specific powers to the federal government, implying that the states retained powers that were not delegated. Nonetheless, he saw no problem with amending the Constitution to make this point obvious.

Since the ratification of the Constitution, the Tenth Amendment has been used by the states to take a number of actions, some of which have been more successful than others.

Nullification

In 1798, Thomas Jefferson argued in his anonymously penned Kentucky Resolutions that the Tenth Amendment enabled a state to nullify congressional legislation that went beyond the scope of the powers delegated by the Constitution. Jefferson was writing in response to the Alien and Sedition Acts, which restricted the press in direct violation of the First Amendment. Thirty years later, South Carolina attempted to nullify the Tariff of 1828, resulting in the Nullification Crisis, which was resolved by a compromise a few years later. Since the Nullification Crisis, no state has directly attempted to void a federal law. Experience has determined that the Supreme Court—not the states—holds this power.

Secession

After Abraham Lincoln was elected president in 1860, Southern politicians cited the Tenth Amendment as justification for secession because the Constitution doesn't prohibit states from leaving the Union. President Lincoln, of course, disagreed with their assessment, declaring that the Constitution creates an indivisible Union. Ultimately, the Civil War settled the secession question in Lincoln's favor. In *Texas v. White* (1869), the Supreme Court affirmed this position, ruling that Texas's ordinance of secession was void because the Union is "indissoluble."

Commandeering

The Tenth Amendment protects the states from federal laws that would require state officials to enforce their provisions, a practice known as commandeering. The Supreme Court affirmed the anti-commandeering principle by prohibiting Congress from forcing the states to pass specific laws or keeping state legislatures from passing laws that they would otherwise pass. In *Murphy v. National Collegiate Athletic Association* (2018), the Court struck down a federal law that barred the states from passing laws regulating sports betting. In the Professional and Amateur Sports Protection Act of 1992, Congress outlawed sports betting throughout the United States while exempting four states that allowed sports betting when the law was passed. Since the Constitution does not give Congress power over sports betting, congressional legislation cannot deny the states the exercise of that power.

"Or to the People"

The phrase "or to the People" did not appear in the original printed draft of the Tenth Amendment that was submitted to Congress. The phrase was added by the hand of the Senate clerk during the congressional debate on the Bill of Rights. Since the Ninth Amendment already protects the people from governmental use of undelegated powers, this phrase at the end of the Tenth Amendment is somewhat redundant.

Cooperative Federalism

While the federal government cannot force states to pass laws, Congress can provide financial incentives to states that pass laws in line with federal preferences. This practice, known as cooperative federalism, entices the states to cooperate voluntarily with federal initiatives. For example, federal law cannot set the drinking age of twenty-one, and the Constitution doesn't grant Congress this authority. In the early 1980s, states set their own drinking ages, which created problems with college students crossing state lines to buy alcohol. To standardize the drinking age across the United States, Congress passed the National Minimum Drinking Age Act in 1984, which offers federal highway funds to states with a drinking age of twenty-one. In the years following the passage of the act, every state set its drinking age to twenty-one to secure federal highway funds.

AMENDING THE CONSTITUTION

Article V of the Constitution designates the states as the only entities empowered to amend the Constitution. While two-thirds of both houses of Congress can propose amendments, an amendment can only be ratified by the consent of three-fourths of the states. Additionally, two-thirds of the states can bypass Congress and call a convention of states to propose amendments to the Constitution. The states have yet to call such a convention.

THE ABOLITION OF SLAVERY

A New Birth of Freedom

The ratification of the Bill of Rights guaranteed the protection of basic rights, although these protections were not granted to everyone at the time. The Constitution has a checkered history, having once functioned as a silent accomplice to slavery in the United States. After decades of protecting slavery in several states, the US terminated slavery once and for all and deemed it a legal form of oppression with the passage of the Thirteenth Amendment.

THE CONSTITUTION AND SLAVERY

The original Constitution represented a compromise not only between large and small states but also between slave states and free states. After the American Revolution, Northern states passed gradual emancipation laws, freeing the few enslaved people they had. The Southern states took no such action, as slavery played a key role in their economy and society. The compromises at the Constitutional Convention guaranteed the protection of slavery as a constitutionally protected institution.

The Apportionment Clause

The Constitution's first tacit acknowledgment of slavery can be found in Article I, Section 2, which states: "Representatives...shall be apportioned among the several States...by adding to the whole Number of free Persons...three fifths of all other Persons." This Three-Fifths Compromise gave the Southern states, whose free white populations were much smaller than the Northern states, greater proportional representation in the House of Representatives.

The International Slave Trade

Article I, Section 9 of the Constitution prohibited Congress from interfering with the international slave trade prior to 1808, giving slave states twenty years to import enslaved people from abroad. Congress passed a law prohibiting the international slave trade in 1808, the first year the Constitution authorized Congress to act. The law passed without any great controversy and was signed into law by President Thomas Jefferson.

The Fugitive Slave Clause

Article IV, Section 2, Clause 3 required all states to cooperate to return fugitives who escaped slavery and sought freedom in another state. It reads:

No Person held to Service or Labour in one State, under the Laws thereof, escaping into another, shall, in Consequence of any Law or Regulation therein, be discharged from such Service or Labour, but shall be delivered up on Claim of the Party to whom such Service or Labour may be due.

—Article IV, Section 2, Clause 3 of the Constitution

Congress enforced the Fugitive Slave Clause with the Fugitive Slave Acts of 1793 and 1850. The Fugitive Slave Act of 1850 created a firestorm of controversy in the United States, as it was passed when the North was turning firmly against slavery.

A Silent Accomplice

Although several clauses of the Constitution protected slavery, the framers were careful never to mention slavery by name. Instead, the Constitution refers to those "held to Service or Labour" or as "all other Persons," following a reference to "free Persons." This omission reflects discomfort with the original Constitution's protections of an institution incompatible with liberty.

ANTISLAVERY MOVEMENTS AND THE CIVIL WAR

By the 1830s, a growing number of Americans believed the Constitution's protections of slavery conflicted with American values of individual liberty and equality. This began decades of sectional debates about slavery that were ultimately resolved by the Civil War.

The Abolitionist Movement

In 1831, William Lloyd Garrison began the abolitionist movement, which sought to immediately abolish slavery throughout the United States, by publishing *The Liberator*, an antislavery newspaper. Garrison's movement gained steam when Frederick Douglass, who had escaped from slavery, published his *Narrative of the Life of Frederick Douglass: An American Slave*, which became an instant bestseller in the North. Abolitionists found common cause with Free Soilers, such as Abraham Lincoln, who opposed the expansion of slavery into the Western territories but did not call for the abolition of slavery in the South.

The Road to Disunion

The antislavery movement grew because of opposition to the passage of the Fugitive Slave Act of 1850, which denied a jury trial to those accused of being fugitives from slavery, and the publication of Harriet Beecher Stowe's *Uncle Tom's Cabin*. When the Supreme Court ruled in *Dred Scott v. Sandford* (1857) that all federal territories must be open to slavery, abolitionists and Free Soilers rose to condemn it. Abraham Lincoln, though not calling for immediate abolition, declared that the United States would eventually have to decide between slavery and freedom.

Lincoln and the Civil War

After Lincoln was elected president, some Southern states seceded. Southern leaders believed that the election of a Republican president would bring about the end of slavery. Early in the Civil War, Lincoln insisted that his only goal was to "preserve the Union" by putting down an insurrection in the Southern states. However, Lincoln's views slowly evolved, starting with the Emancipation Proclamation, which freed enslaved people in states actively rebelling against the United States (while preserving slavery in the pro-Union "border states" and in Confederate areas under Union occupation). Lincoln issued the Emancipation Proclamation as a "necessary war measure" to ensure a Union victory. For Lincoln, this was an important loophole, as the Constitution did not give the president the general power to free enslaved people.

THE THIRTEENTH AMENDMENT

Lincoln worried that the Emancipation Proclamation might be rejected by the courts if the Constitution continued to condone slavery.

Having promised the nation a "new birth of freedom" in the Gettysburg Address, Lincoln worked with Congress to propose a constitutional amendment abolishing slavery forever. On January 31, 1865, Congress passed the Thirteenth Amendment, which bans slavery and involuntary servitude throughout the United States. The amendment was ratified in December, receiving support even from several Southern states that had previously been part of the Confederacy.

THE LONG SHADOW OF SLAVERY

Although the Thirteenth Amendment abolished slavery, its immediate impact on the everyday lives of African Americans was limited for over a century. The Fourteenth Amendment declared formerly enslaved people to be US citizens entitled to equal protection of the laws, and the Fifteenth Amendment prohibited voter discrimination based on race, color, or previous condition of servitude. However, Southern states responded with "Jim Crow" laws, which limited the rights of these new citizens. The Supreme Court's *Plessy v. Ferguson* (1896) decision allowed racial segregation in public facilities as long as there were "separate but equal" accommodations for both races. Over fifty years later, the Court overturned *Plessy* in its unanimous *Brown v. Board of Education* (1954) decision.

Even today, debates continue regarding the extent to which the United States remains under the shadow of slavery. In 2020, the murder of George Floyd sparked protests concerning systemic inequalities that still affect African Americans today. Over 150 years after its ratification, the Thirteenth Amendment reflects an important milestone in an ongoing national struggle to live up to the ideals expressed in the Declaration of Independence.

THE RIGHT TO VOTE

A Right and Responsibility of Citizenship

The right to vote is treasured by many Americans. Republicanism itself is dependent upon elected leaders being supported by the voting public. In today's American democratic republic, this right is exercised by every citizen over the age of eighteen. However, this consensus concerning voting is relatively recent in the grand scheme of American history, having been established by the Twenty-Sixth Amendment in 1971. Between the ratification of the Constitution and the passage of the Twenty-Sixth Amendment, voting has slowly evolved from being a privilege for white male property owners to a right exercised by any adult American who chooses to do so.

VOTING IN EARLY NATIONAL AMERICA

Although Article IV, Section 4 of the Constitution guarantees every state a republican form of government with elections for public officials, the voting public is not defined. In the early republic, each state determined qualifications for its voters. Perhaps unsurprisingly, no state in the early republic allowed women to vote. Not only could enslaved people not vote; most states (even in the North) did not consider free people of color to be worthy of exercising the most basic right of citizenship. White men were also not guaranteed the right to vote, as state constitutions required voters to own property.

"JACKSONIAN" DEMOCRACY

Between 1824 and 1840, the United States transitioned from an aristocratic republic into a democratic republic, which presumed all white men to be equals in the political community. As states west of the Appalachian Mountains entered the Union, their constitutions included suffrage for all white men. Andrew Jackson, whose name is often attached to this expansion of democracy in the early nineteenth century, prided himself on being a "self-made" man who attained the presidency in spite of being born outside of the political elite.

Suffrage and the Franchise

Over the years, voting rights have been described in different terms, with campaigns to expand voting rights referring to "suffrage" and the "elective franchise." Suffrage is drawn from the Latin *suffragium*, which is how the ancient Romans referred to a voting tablet; franchise comes from the Old French *franchir*, a verb meaning "to free."

By the 1840s, nearly all states had removed property requirements for voting. While this demonstrated progress toward universal suffrage, it still excluded women and nonwhite populations. The 1848 Seneca Falls Declaration of Sentiments protested the exclusion of women, criticizing state governments that continued to "with[hold] from her rights which are given to the most ignorant and degraded men."

THE RECONSTRUCTION AMENDMENTS

After the Civil War, the Constitution was amended three times in order to further the cause of racial equality in the United States. The three amendments are as follows:

- **The Thirteenth Amendment** abolished slavery, but it did not clarify the citizenship status of freed men and women.
- **The Fourteenth Amendment** conferred birthright citizenship on all Americans (overturning *Dred Scott*), but it did not tie citizenship to the right to vote. Section 2 of the Fourteenth Amendment authorizes Congress to cut a state's congressional representation if the state disenfranchises any male inhabitants. This section was designed to discourage Southern states from denying African Americans the right to vote.
  - Section 2 also enabled states to deny people the right to vote "for participation in rebellion, or other crime." States retain the authority to determine which convicted criminals forfeit their voting rights. For example, in Maine and Vermont, felons can vote during their prison terms, while in Tennessee and Wyoming, convicted felons can't vote for life. Most states are somewhere in between these extremes, restoring voting privileges after incarceration.
- **The Fifteenth Amendment** prohibits both the federal and state governments from denying anyone the right to vote "on account of race, color, or previous condition of servitude." The Fifteenth Amendment took an important step in preventing racial discrimination in voting, but many states (especially those in the South) found ways around the amendment's prohibitions of racial discrimination in voting, which included the following:

- **Poll taxes:** Some states required voters to pay poll taxes prior to voting. These taxes were designed to prevent both African Americans and poor white people in the South from voting.
- **Literacy tests:** Some states used literacy tests to keep African Americans, poor white people, and recent immigrants from voting.
- **Grandfather clauses:** Some states, when passing laws creating poll taxes and literacy tests, exempted people who could vote (as well as their descendants) at the time that the laws were passed. These "grandfather clauses" denied voting rights to formerly enslaved people, whose grandfathers had been ineligible to vote.
- **Voter intimidation:** Black Americans in the South who asserted their right to vote risked being intimidated by the Ku Klux Klan.

WOMEN'S SUFFRAGE

The passage of the Fifteenth Amendment caused a division in the women's rights movement, as many objected to the continued exclusion of women. Frederick Douglass, the great antislavery campaigner who had been present at the Seneca Falls Convention in 1848, advocated for women's suffrage. He, however, supported the Fifteenth Amendment because it wouldn't have had a chance of ratification if it had included women's suffrage.

In the late nineteenth century, women's suffrage advocates experienced successes at the state level, especially in Western states. In 1869, Wyoming Territory became the first in US jurisdiction to recognize equal voting rights for men and women.

World War I increased support for women's suffrage throughout the developed world. In 1920, the United States ratified the Nineteenth Amendment to the Constitution, which declared: "The right of citizens of the United States to vote shall not be denied or abridged by the United States or by any State on account of sex."

THE CIVIL RIGHTS ERA

In the 1960s, the civil rights movement led to Congress addressing the voter suppression and discrimination that African Americans were still facing a century after the passage of the Thirteenth Amendment. "The Negro still is not free," the Reverend Martin Luther King Jr. observed in his "I Have a Dream" speech in 1963. In 1964, the states ratified the Twenty-Fourth Amendment, which prohibited states from requiring poll taxes. In 1965, Congress passed the Voting Rights Act, allowing the federal government to oversee elections in states with histories of voter discrimination.

THE VIETNAM ERA

In the late 1960s, college students protested the Vietnam War draft. They argued that it was unfair to draft people who could not vote. The Twenty-Sixth Amendment, ratified in 1971, guarantees voting rights at the age of eighteen.

VOTING RIGHTS IN
CONTEMPORARY AMERICA

Discussions continue in contemporary America regarding voting rights, election security, and voter suppression. The states still decide many of their own election procedures, such as access to early voting and whether voters are required to show identification to vote. Advocates for voter identification claim that it is necessary to ensure the integrity of elections, while critics claim that it is a form of voter suppression that disproportionately impacts many of the same demographic categories of voters who were once barred from voting by poll taxes and literacy tests. Additionally, some states allow seventeen-year-olds to vote in party primaries if they are eighteen by the time of the general election.

Chapter 3

The Legislative Branch

Having explored the many ways in which the amended Constitution protects the rights of Americans, it's time to focus on the original Constitution, which organizes the federal government and determines the extent of its powers. Taking a cue from the French political philosopher, Montesquieu, the framers chose to separate the powers of the federal government between three branches: legislative, executive, and judicial.

Article I of the Constitution outlines the legislative power of the federal government. Of the three branches, the legislative branch is the most important in a democratic republic because it is the branch in which the people's representatives gather to make laws. Laws must first be made before they can be enforced or judged. This is why the legislative branch is the first of the branches to be organized under the Constitution.

THE LEGISLATIVE POWER

The Creation of the US Congress

Immediately after the Preamble, the main body of the Constitution begins with Article I, focusing on the powers, organization, and elections of the members of the legislative branch of government. The Constitution's first order of business is to invest legislative authority in the US Congress.

> All legislative Powers herein granted shall be vested in a Congress of the United States, which shall consist of a Senate and House of Representatives.
>
> —Article I, Section 1 of the Constitution

WHAT IS A CONGRESS?

Today, it is rare for Americans to use the word *congress* outside of making a direct reference to the US Congress, but the word used to refer to formal gatherings of delegates who discussed important matters. The Latin words from which *congress* is derived literally mean to "come together" or "walk together." Nowadays, the US Congress provides a forum for representatives to discuss important national matters.

CONGRESSES BEFORE THE CONSTITUTION

The designation of the federal legislature as Congress drew on historical gatherings of delegates representing the colonies (and later states) before, during, and after the American Revolution. These congresses enabled Americans to speak with one voice rather than thirteen.

The Stamp Act Congress

After the British Parliament passed the Stamp Act in 1765, representatives from nine of the thirteen British colonies met in New York City to express their grievances against Parliament's taxation of the colonies without the consent of their representatives in the colonial legislatures. The Stamp Act Congress was an informal meeting with no legal status.

The Continental Congresses

In 1774, the First Continental Congress met to draft resolutions and petitions in response to the Intolerable Acts, which had been passed by Parliament after the Boston Tea Party. After the battles of Lexington and Concord in 1775, the Second Continental Congress convened to organize a common defense for the thirteen colonies. It was the members of the Second Continental Congress that signed the Declaration of Independence in 1776.

The Confederation Congress

The Articles of Confederation, ratified by the states in 1781, vested federal authority in a unicameral (one-house) Congress. Since the Articles did not create an independent executive branch, members of the Confederation Congress had to perform executive functions too.

THE US CONGRESS

The framers of the Constitution also granted legislative authority to a Congress, but with a new structure and several new powers. The

Congress was carefully designed to encourage consensus and keep any faction from controlling the legislative process.

A Bicameral Legislature

The Constitution created a bicameral (two-house) legislature, consisting of a Senate and a House of Representatives. While the division of legislative power between two houses was partly due to the Great Compromise between the large and small states at the Constitutional Convention, the framers partly had a strategic goal of balancing the powers of the three branches of government. In Federalist No. 51, James Madison explained that separating Congress into two houses was necessary to keep the legislative branch from excessively weakening the executive branch.

Unlike the Congress established by the articles, the Congress established by the Constitution was intended to be one of three branches of government, which would pass laws that were to be enforced by a chief executive whose powers were independent of Congress.

The States and the People

The bicameral nature of Congress also captures the nature of the US government, which operates in some respects as a union of states and in others as a national government unifying the American people as a whole. Just as the ancient Romans had been governed by "The Senate and the People of Rome," the United States would be governed by the Senate, representing the states, and the House, representing the people.

Aristocracy and Democracy

Initially, the Senate and the House had different modes of election, with senators being appointed by state legislatures and representatives in the House being elected directly by voters. While the framers believed that the government created by the Constitution should have democratic elements, they did not seek to create a government that was fully democratic. They were influenced by Greek philosopher Aristotle, who believed that an effective government balanced the interests of property owners with the interests of the people, at large.

The Virginia Plan

The original Constitution provided for the appointment of senators by the state legislatures; however, James Madison's Virginia Plan called for the senators to be elected by the members of the House of Representatives. Both the Virginia Plan and the original Constitution reflected the framers' skepticism about letting voters directly elect members of both houses of Congress.

Individuals with Fixed Terms

The Constitution altered the dynamics of Congress, giving its members individual seats with fixed terms of office. Under the Articles of Confederation, state legislatures can change the composition of their state delegations, substituting members at any time. Under the Constitution, states may not recall members of Congress during their terms. If citizens do not like the way their senators or representatives are representing them, they must wait until the next election to replace them.

THE LEGISLATIVE PROCESS

In order for any piece of legislation to become law, both the Senate and the House must pass identical versions of a bill by a majority vote before sending it to the president to be signed into law. In the case of a presidential veto, the Senate and the House must pass the legislation again by a two-thirds vote of each house.

THE HOUSE OF REPRESENTATIVES

The House of the People

The US House of Representatives, currently composed of 435 members, is the "lower house" of Congress, in which each state is represented in proportion to its population. The House of Representatives embodies the nationalizing aspect of the Constitution. It is the house of "We the People."

THE PEOPLE'S HOUSE

In Federalist No. 52, James Madison described the House of Representatives as "that branch of the federal government which ought to be dependent on the people alone." Under the original Constitution, the House was the only part of the federal government whose members were elected by a direct vote of the people. Although the framers didn't trust the idea of a pure democracy, they believed that the government created by the Constitution must have a strong democratic element to avoid becoming a pure aristocracy. The House of Representatives forms a democratic counterweight to the comparatively aristocratic Senate.

SPECIAL POWERS OF THE HOUSE

The House of Representatives has several distinct powers that the Senate cannot exercise: initiating revenue bills, drafting articles of impeachment, and electing the president when the Electoral College fails to do so.

Revenue Bills

Article I, Section 7 of the Constitution gives the House of Representatives the sole power to initiate revenue bills (bills that concern taxation). This provision comes from the revolutionary struggle against "taxation without representation." The power to fund the government is important because it also gives the House an important check against the Senate and the president. Although the House depends on the Senate and the president to pass legislation, the Senate and the president depend on the House to fund the government.

Articles of Impeachment

The House of Representatives has the sole power to initiate the impeachment process (charging a public official with misconduct) against federal officials. An impeachment begins when the House approves articles of impeachment by a majority vote. After the House approves these articles, they are sent to the Senate, where impeachment trials are conducted in accordance with the Constitution.

Contingent Elections

The Constitution also gives the House the power to elect the president if no candidate receives a majority vote from the Electoral College. In an interesting twist, when the House elects the president in a contingent election, the members do not vote by head. They vote, instead, by state delegations, with the candidate supported by the majority of each state's delegation receiving one vote. If a contingent election were held in the House today, a presidential candidate would need the support of twenty-six state delegations to be elected.

CONSTITUTIONAL QUALIFICATIONS FOR REPRESENTATIVES

To qualify for election to the House of Representatives, a person must be at least twenty-five years of age, a US citizen for at least seven years, and a resident of the state in which they are running. Curiously, House members don't need to live in the district they are representing. While voters generally prefer to be represented by people living in their district, a representative may sometimes be drawn out of their district during redistricting after a federal census. Additionally, since some large cities have several congressional districts, representatives may live outside of their represented district but still within the city itself.

ELECTIONS AND TERMS OF OFFICE

While the Constitution does not give a set criterion for voting qualifications, it does mandate in Article I, Section 2 that the qualifications for voting for the House of Representatives should be identical to that of the "most numerous Branch of the State Legislature." This guarantees that if someone is eligible to vote in a state legislative election, they would also be able to vote for their congressional representatives. The framers wanted to keep states from making the qualifications to vote for the House any stricter than the requirements to vote in state elections.

A House term is set at two years, shorter than those of the president and senators. The shorter terms are designed to make the House more directly accountable to the people, as these representatives must answer to the voters more often than anyone else in the federal government. However, many Antifederalists argued that Roman-style annual (yearly) elections were necessary in order to make the House dependent on the people. Madison countered this argument in Federalist No. 53, reasoning that a one-year term would not give House members enough time to learn to do their jobs properly. The Constitution was ratified with the two-term period intact.

Gerrymandering

Because the state legislatures determine the boundaries of House districts, these district boundaries are often "gerrymandered" in favor of the dominant party. Gerrymandering occurs when district boundaries are intentionally drawn to provide an advantage for one political party. Although controversial, it is not unconstitutional. Furthermore, gerrymandering can offer some advantages, such as ensuring that ethnic minorities receive representation in Congress. In *Shaw v. Reno* (1993), the Supreme Court upheld the constitutionality of the intentional creation of majority-minority districts, as long as these districts were drawn in a sensible fashion.

The Original Gerrymander

In 1812, Governor Elbridge Gerry of Massachusetts signed a bill that created congressional districts that heavily favored Thomas Jefferson's Democratic-Republican Party. Members of the Federalist Party protested, comparing one of the Boston-area districts to a salamander. In doing so, they created a new mythical creature that became known as the "Gerrymander."

Political Polarization

Gerrymandering has increased the level of political polarization in the House of Representatives because it creates districts that favor Democratic or Republican candidates. The partisan makeup of these districts encourages candidates to appeal to more extreme elements within their parties since the minority party in the district lacks credible voting power.

HOUSE OFFICERS

The only officer of the House of Representatives mentioned in the Constitution is the Speaker of the House, who acts as the House's presiding officer. Although the Speaker of the House has always been a member of the House of Representatives, the House could theoretically elect a Speaker who is not a member of the House. In 2023, when Republicans could not decide on a Speaker, former president Donald Trump was suggested as a potential candidate for the position (this never came to a vote).

THE US SENATE

The Senate of the United States, currently made up of one hundred members, is the "upper house" of Congress, in which every state is represented by two senators. The Senate embodies the federal nature of the government created by the Constitution, giving all states an equal voice regardless of population.

AN AUGUST BODY

As the upper house of Congress, the Senate was intended to be an august (dignified) body, conducting its business with the dignity and courtesy that once defined the Roman Senate. Even today, it's common for a senator to refer to another formally as "the senator from Illinois" rather than directly by name. These traditions of courtesy contrast the Senate with the less formal House of Representatives.

UNLIMITED DEBATE

With only one hundred members, the Senate does not have to limit its floor debates as much as the larger House of Representatives. While House members must confine their remarks to shorter time limits, senators have the floor for as long as they wish. Sometimes, this tradition that embodies the courtesy of the Senate can be used to delay votes on legislation in the form of a filibuster.

The Filibuster

A filibuster occurs when either a single senator or a group of senators opposes a piece of legislation so strongly that they give a long speech (or speeches) to keep the legislation from coming to a vote. To be effective, a filibuster must have the support of at least forty-one senators, but even one senator may delay the vote on a piece of legislation for a day with a long speech.

Senator Strom Thurmond of South Carolina set the record for the longest single-person filibuster in Senate history by holding the floor for twenty-four hours and eighteen minutes in opposition to the Civil Rights Act of 1957. Thurmond's speech included readings from Supreme Court decisions and Washington's Farewell Address. In 2013, Senator Ted Cruz of Texas gave a twenty-one-hour speech that included a dramatic reading of Dr. Seuss's *Green Eggs and Ham* as a bedtime story for his daughters.

The Senate's cloture rule and accompanying filibusters are often criticized for allowing a minority faction to hold up Senate business (including pieces of legislation with majority support); however, defenders of this tradition note that it ensures that legislation only passes the Senate when a consensus is reached.

Cloture

Cloture is a procedure used by legislators to defeat a filibuster. Sixteen senators can call for a vote to limit or end the debate; it takes sixty votes (or three-fifths majority) to approve a motion for cloture. Once invoked, legislators have a maximum of thirty additional hours to debate a proposal.

SPECIAL POWERS OF THE SENATE

In addition to the Senate's standard legislative functions, the framers gave it a number of special responsibilities and powers that it exercises independently from the House. These unique powers give the Senate important checks on the executive and judicial branches.

Confirming Presidential Nominees

All federal officials nominated for office by the president, including all cabinet members, foreign ambassadors, and federal judges, must be confirmed by the Senate. In recent decades, Senate debates over Supreme Court nominees have become increasingly contentious—each party seeks to control the composition of the Court.

Ratifying Treaties

All treaties must be ratified by a two-thirds vote of the Senate. Article II of the Constitution directs the president to seek the "advice and consent" of the Senate. This means that senators are not only involved in ratifying treaties; they should also take an advisory role during treaty negotiations.

Impeachment Proceedings

Whenever the House of Representatives initiates the impeachment process by voting in favor of articles of impeachment, the Senate conducts the impeachment trial, with senators acting as the jury. Two-thirds of senators must vote for a guilty verdict in order to remove an impeached official from office.

Mr. Smith Goes to Washington

Mr. Smith Goes to Washington, a beloved cinematic classic, is a 1939 film starring Jimmy Stewart as an average guy named Jefferson Smith who is appointed by the governor to finish the term of a deceased senator. The film gives some insight into Senate traditions and depicts the Senate as a stifled body out of touch with everyday Americans.

CONSTITUTIONAL QUALIFICATIONS FOR SENATORS

To be eligible for election to the Senate, a person must meet three specific criteria outlined in the Constitution: They must be at least thirty years old, have been a citizen of the United States for at least nine years, and reside in the state they wish to represent at the time of their election.

ELECTIONS AND TERMS OF OFFICE

Senators serve for six-year terms of office, reflecting the desire of the framers for the Senate to be a stable body not affected by short-lived popular whims. Every two years, a third of the senators are up for reelection, preserving a measure of continuity even in years of wave elections dominated by one party. Originally, the Constitution called for senators to be appointed by state legislatures to create some distance between senators and the general electorate; however, this changed with the ratification of the Seventeenth Amendment in 1913, requiring senators to be elected by a popular vote of a state's citizens.

SENATE OFFICERS

The Constitution designates that the vice president of the United States shall serve as the president of the Senate. The vice president, being part of the executive branch (and not a member of the Senate), is not able to cast a vote in the Senate except to break a tie. The Constitution also requires the Senate to elect a president pro tempore (for the time being), who will preside over the Senate when the vice president is unable to do so. Traditionally, the position of president pro tempore is occupied by the longest-serving senator from the majority party.

THE TAXING POWER

Funding the Federal Government

In granting Congress the power to tax, the framers remedied a key defect in the Articles of Confederation. Under the Articles, Congress was able to assess (request) taxes from the states but had no authority to collect them. This made it difficult for the federal government to fund foreign relations and national defense. In addition, the lack of taxing power meant that Congress had no means of paying down the national debt from the Revolutionary War. The Constitution's taxing power ensures the fulfillment of these important responsibilities.

ANTIFEDERALIST OBJECTIONS

During the debates over ratification, some Antifederalists argued against giving Congress the taxing power, fearing that both state and federal governments having such power would lead to an intolerable tax burden. "In this scheme of energetic government," said Patrick Henry of Virginia, "the people will find two sets of tax-gatherers—the state and the federal sheriffs." Ultimately, the Antifederalists were unsuccessful in maintaining the old system of federal requisitions from the states.

THE TAXING POWER

The Congress shall have Power To lay and collect Taxes, Duties, Imposts and Excises, to pay the Debts and provide for the common Defence and general Welfare of the United States; but all

Duties, Imposts and Excises shall be uniform throughout the United States.

—Article I, Section 8, Clause 1 of the Constitution

As seen in the aforementioned quote, the Constitution delegates the taxing power to Congress. In placing the taxation power in the hands of Congress, the Constitution gives the legislative branch "the power of the purse" as a check on the executive branch. Although the president operates independently of Congress in the day-to-day operations of the government, the president is dependent on Congress to fund the operations of the executive branch. As mentioned earlier, the Constitution also gives the House of Representatives the sole power to initiate bills to raise revenue, ensuring that the people are taxed directly by their representatives and not "without representation" as had been done under British rule. While the Senate cannot initiate revenue bills, it can offer amendments to tax legislation.

TYPES OF FEDERAL TAXES

Over the years, the federal government has raised revenue in a variety of ways under the Constitution, including excise taxes, tariffs, and income taxes. Each provides money to the government (though some much more than others).

Excise Taxes

The Constitution empowers the federal government to raise excise taxes, which are taxes on the sale or manufacture of goods and services. During George Washington's administration, Treasury Secretary Alexander Hamilton persuaded Congress to pass an excise tax on whiskey that was met with rebellion. During Thomas Jefferson's presidency, Hamilton's excise tax was eliminated, as the cost of paying people to collect the tax exceeded the revenue it produced.

Today, the federal government collects excise taxes in the form of sales taxes on gasoline and diesel fuel, passenger airline tickets, tobacco products, and alcoholic beverages. Unlike state sales taxes, which are tacked onto the total, these federal taxes are generally included in the price of the taxed goods. Excise taxes currently make up only a small share of federal revenue, with less than 2 percent of federal internal revenues coming from excises in 2022. Sales taxes form a higher share of state revenues, with forty-five states collecting at least some share of revenue through sales taxes.

The 9–9–9 Plan

In 2011, Herman Cain, a former CEO who sought the Republican nomination for president, proposed to revive the excise tax as a major source of federal revenue. His 9–9–9 Plan would have instituted a 9 percent federal sales tax, which would have been offset by lowering personal and corporate income tax rates to 9 percent.

Tariffs

During the nineteenth century, tariffs (referenced in the Constitution as "duties") made up the largest portion of federal revenue. A tariff is a tax on imported goods, collected when goods enter the country. Tariffs can be broadly classified into two categories: revenue and protective. Revenue tariffs are low and collected for the sole purpose of funding the government, while protective tariffs are typically higher and passed to discourage imports (thereby "protecting" domestic industries from foreign competition). Although South Carolina attempted to challenge the constitutionality of protective tariffs during the Nullification Crisis, the Supreme Court has never ruled them to be unconstitutional. Protective tariffs are a rarity today, as free trade policies have become common with increasing globalization.

Income Taxes

In the late nineteenth century, Southern and Western farmers campaigned against high protective tariffs, which they believed helped the manufacturing sector at their expense. They campaigned for replacing tariff revenue with a federal income tax that would be paid by wealthy Americans. The Revenue Act of 1894 included a modest 2 percent income tax that would be paid by a small number of Americans with large incomes. The Supreme Court struck down the income tax imposed by this act in *Pollock v. Farmers' Loan & Trust Company* (1895), ruling in a controversial 5–4 decision that the 1894 income tax was unconstitutional because it taxed people directly in a way that was not "uniform throughout the United States" as required by the Constitution.

In response to the *Pollock* decision, Congress proposed the Sixteenth Amendment, which gave Congress the power "to lay and collect taxes on incomes...without apportionment among the several States." The states ratified the Sixteenth Amendment in 1913, and Congress quickly responded by passing a federal income tax and lowering tariffs. Since the 1940s, the majority of federal revenues have come from income taxes.

LIMITATIONS ON THE TAXING POWER

The power to tax is not an unlimited power; Congress can assess taxes to "pay the Debts and provide for the common Defence and general Welfare of the United States." However, the Supreme Court has generally upheld an expansive view of the federal taxation power. In *United States v. Butler* (1936), the Court ruled that Congress has broad powers to tax on the basis of providing for the general welfare. However, in the same decision, the Court struck down the Agricultural Adjustment Act of 1933 by ruling that it was not an actual tax but rather an attempt to regulate agriculture at the federal level, thus infringing on the reserved powers of the states. Congress cannot use a federal tax or subsidy as a means to restrict the states from exercising their reserved powers. A few examples of these taxing restrictions follow.

- **Exports:** Article I, Section 9 of the Constitution prohibits Congress from taxing exports. This is why goods sold at duty-free stores in US international airports are not taxed, as the people purchasing the goods are leaving the country, thereby "exporting" the goods from the United States.
- **Property taxes:** Since the income tax is the only form of federal taxation that is exempt from the constitutional requirement that taxes be assessed uniformly, the vast difference in property values from state to state would make a federal property tax unworkable under the Constitution.

BORROWING MONEY

Managing the National Debt

One of the most pressing problems facing the framers of the Constitution was the massive public debt from the Revolutionary War. Without the taxing power, the Confederation Congress had trouble financing even the government's necessary operations. Revolutionary War veterans and foreign creditors who had helped finance the war remained unpaid. Alexander Hamilton conveyed the desperate state of federal finances in *The Federalist Papers*.

> We may indeed with propriety be said to have reached almost the last stage of national humiliation....Do we owe debts to foreigners and to our own citizens contracted in a time of imminent peril for the preservation of our political existence? These remain without any proper or satisfactory provision for their discharge.
>
> —Federalist No. 15 (Hamilton)

The framers sought to remedy the United States' desperate financial situation by granting Congress the power to borrow money and manage the federal debt.

THE BORROWING POWER

The borrowing power is the second of the enumerated powers of Congress found in Article I, Section 8 of the Constitution, appearing directly after the taxing power. The Constitution empowers Congress "to borrow Money on the credit of the United States." Unlike the taxing power, the borrowing power was nothing new, as the Articles of Confederation had also authorized Congress to borrow money. In fact, the borrowing power is one power that was trimmed back by the framers, as the Articles of Confederation enabled Congress to "borrow money or emit bills on the credit of the United States." The convention removed authorization for Congress to emit bills of credit, as the framers wanted Congress to discontinue printing paper money in order to satisfy debts.

The Constitution states that the federal government will not only borrow money but will also reliably pay back any borrowed funds. This guarantee applies to the debts of the United States contracted before the Constitution was ratified. Article VI of the Constitution guarantees that Congress will maintain responsibility for the repayment of all outstanding debts from the Confederation period. "All Debts contracted and Engagements entered into, before the Adoption of this Constitution," it reads, "shall be as valid against the United States under this Constitution, as under the Confederation."

HAMILTON'S REPORT ON THE PUBLIC CREDIT

When George Washington selected Alexander Hamilton as the nation's first secretary of the treasury, he gave him the unenviable task of devising a plan to manage the large national debt. Hamilton rose to the occasion, presenting his First Report on the Public Credit to Congress in 1790. The report was extremely ambitious, calling for the payment of the outstanding national debt at face value (rather than settling with creditors for a percentage of the outstanding debt) to the current holders of the debt certificates. Unfortunately, many Continental Army veterans who were paid with paper Continental notes during the Revolutionary War had sold their notes to currency speculators for pennies on the dollar, believing they would never be able to exchange them for hard currency. Furthermore, Hamilton proposed that the federal government assume all of the remaining war debts that were owed by the state governments.

Thomas Jefferson and James Madison took issue with Hamilton's plan because it would reward currency speculators while leaving war veterans unpaid. Their native state of Virginia was also one of a handful of states that had already paid off its war debts. However, they agreed to support Hamilton's plan in exchange for his support for a permanent federal capital on the Potomac River, giving the Virginians proximity to the seat of government. The so-called Dinner Table Compromise, having been reached at a dinner hosted by Jefferson, paved the way for the new government to build sound public credit.

THE FOURTEENTH AMENDMENT

Section 4 of the Fourteenth Amendment states: "The validity of the public debt of the United States...shall not be questioned." This was largely meant to uphold the public debt that the United States incurred during the Civil War while at the same time prohibiting any debts owed by the Confederate government from ever being paid. Section 4 is occasionally mentioned by politicians during debates in Congress about raising the debt ceiling, but the Supreme Court has never ruled concerning whether Section 4 prohibits Congress from defaulting on (refusing to pay or finance) the national debt.

The Deficit and the Debt

A budget deficit (or surplus) refers to an annual budget in which the government spends more (or less) money in a fiscal year than it collected in taxes, while the national debt refers to the total amount of money that the government owes to creditors. The national debt is the result of the accumulation of budget deficits over the years.

NO BALANCED BUDGET REQUIREMENT

The Constitution does not limit federal borrowing, nor does it require Congress to balance its budget by keeping the federal government's spending below its tax revenues. In recent years, the Constitution's lack of a borrowing limit has become a concern, as Congress has gotten into the habit of spending much more than it receives in taxes. The four balanced budgets between 1998 and 2001 are the exception to over fifty years of deficit spending. These budget deficits have accumulated to create a national debt of over $34 trillion. Ever since the 1990s, there have been calls for a "balanced budget" amendment that would require Congress to pass balanced budgets during peacetime. However, such an amendment has never received the required two-thirds support from both houses of Congress that would send it to the states for consideration. The growing national debt remains a matter of major concern, as Democrats and Republicans have been unable to agree to taxation and spending policies that would result in a balanced federal budget. The Constitution provides no automatic remedy.

THE COMMERCE CLAUSE

Regulating Foreign and Interstate Trade

The Declaration of Independence established the former thirteen colonies as "free and independent states," allowing these independent states to "levy War, conclude Peace, contract Alliances, [and] establish Commerce." While the Articles of Confederation clearly placed the powers of war, peace, and alliances in the hands of Congress, regulating commerce was left in the hands of the states. After winning independence from Britain, the states were hesitant to delegate the control of their commerce to any outside authority. However, the arrangement in the Articles created a chaotic free-for-all, in which each state set its own tariff rates for imports and could even place tariffs on goods imported from other states. To remedy this problem, the framers placed the Commerce Clause into the Constitution to ensure free trade between the states and a uniform regulation of foreign trade.

THE COMMERCE CLAUSE

The Commerce Clause of the Constitution reads:

> The Congress shall have Power....To regulate Commerce with foreign Nations, and among the several States, and with the Indian Tribes.
>
> —Article I, Section 8, Clause 3 of the Constitution

This clause gives Congress control of foreign trade, commercial relations with Native American tribes, and interstate commerce that passes between states. It also affirms the principle of federalism by placing the states in control of regulating commerce that does not cross state lines.

WHAT IS INTERSTATE COMMERCE?

Although the states are clearly excluded from regulating foreign trade and commerce with Native American tribes, a precise definition of what commerce "among the several states" includes is ambiguous. The meaning of the Commerce Clause can vary widely depending on whether it's given a narrow or broad reading.

The Narrow Reading

When read narrowly, the Commerce Clause applies to commercial transactions that have a direct effect on interstate commerce, such as shipping goods across state lines or operating an online business that has customers in several states. Advocates of a narrow reading of the Commerce Clause, who tend to be politically conservative, emphasize the limitations of the congressional regulatory power and the original intent of the framers, who wrote the Commerce Clause to prohibit states from imposing tariffs on each other.

The Broad Reading

A broad reading of the Commerce Clause gives Congress the power to regulate commercial transactions that have both a direct and an indirect effect on interstate commerce. Advocates of a broad reading of the Commerce Clause, who tend to be politically liberal, emphasize the increasing nationalization of the US economy as a justification for Congress to have expansive regulatory powers. It's hard today to find a business transaction that does not, in some way, impact people in other states. The broad reading of the Commerce Clause is most compatible with the theory of a "living Constitution" that changes with the times.

REGULATION OF TRANSPORTATION

The original Constitution does not specifically address the modern transportation industry, as planes, trains, and automobiles did not exist at the time of its writing. State and federal regulatory powers have needed to be clarified as transportation technologies have advanced. At the turn of the nineteenth century, the steamboat revolutionized transportation, allowing ships to carry passengers and freight upriver for the first time. Robert Fulton, who introduced steamboats in the United States, got a twenty-year monopoly for operating steamboats in New York. When Thomas Gibbons began carrying steamboat passengers between New York City and Elizabeth, New Jersey, Aaron Ogden sued him. Ogden, who held a state license to operate the route, received a favorable verdict in a New York court, and Gibbons was forced to shut down his operation in the state.

Gibbons appealed the ruling to the US Supreme Court, which ruled in his favor on the basis of the Commerce Clause, which gives Congress the sole power to regulate any commerce that passes from state to state. The *Gibbons v. Ogden* (1824) decision established that interstate transportation is included in the Constitution's definition of commerce and that Congress has the sole right to regulate it. This cleared the way for the eventual federal regulation of the railroad and aviation industries.

"The Commodore"

In addition to being at the center of a major Supreme Court case, Thomas Gibbons made a profound impact on the history of the United States when he hired young Cornelius Vanderbilt to captain one of his steamboats. Vanderbilt, known as "the Commodore," built a fortune revolutionizing shipping and railroad transportation.

Although Congress exclusively regulates interstate transportation, the states retain the right to regulate local transportation, such as taxis and rideshares (Uber and Lyft), which typically offer rides to passengers within a single city or state. State departments of transportation also have some leeway to regulate commercial drivers' licenses within general guidelines set by the Federal Motor Carrier Safety Administration.

THE COMMERCE CLAUSE
AND THE NEW DEAL

In the 1930s, President Franklin D. Roosevelt (FDR) launched his New Deal programs, bringing federal interventions into economic matters that had previously been regulated by the states or private enterprise. One of these programs was the National Industrial Recovery Act (NIRA), which created regulatory codes for private businesses regardless of whether these businesses operated across state lines. In a specific case, federal regulators clashed with the Schechter brothers, who operated a local kosher butchery in New York City. The regulators attempted to micromanage the Schechters' locally owned business by not allowing customers to pick which chicken they wanted butchered. When the Schechters defied the federal regulatory agents, they were criminally charged. The Schechters then petitioned the Supreme Court to hear their case. In *Schechter Poultry Corp. v. United States* (1935), the Supreme Court unanimously struck down the NIRA as unconstitutional on the following grounds:

1. The NIRA had improperly delegated legislative power to the executive branch by allowing an executive branch agency to draw up business regulations.
2. Since the Schechters' business sold poultry to local clients, their business dealings did not directly affect interstate commerce and couldn't be restricted by the federal government.

President Roosevelt, displeased, accused the Supreme Court of using a "horse-and-buggy definition of interstate commerce" to arrive at its ruling. The tensions between the president and the Supreme Court became so great that FDR came up with a "court-packing plan" that would have enabled him to increase the number of justices on the Supreme Court if Congress had not rejected it. However, these tensions subsided a few years later when the Court upheld the National Labor Relations Act, which gave the federal government broad new powers to protect the rights of laborers to form unions.

BROADENING THE COMMERCE CLAUSE

In the 1960s, Congress passed sweeping new legislation that supported the goals of the civil rights movement. The Civil Rights Act of 1964 prohibited any discrimination based on race, color, religion, sex, and national origin by schools, employers, and owners of public accommodations. This act was an unprecedented federal regulation of private business transactions (including transactions that did not directly cross state lines). In *Heart of Atlanta Motel v. United States* (1964), the Supreme Court unanimously upheld the Civil Rights Act of 1964, ruling that the Heart of Atlanta Motel could not refuse to offer rooms to those who identify as Black. The Court noted that given the motel's location along interstate highways, it participated indirectly in interstate commerce, as many guests were out-of-state travelers.

NARROWING THE COMMERCE CLAUSE

In recent decades, the Supreme Court has moved toward narrowing its reading of the Commerce Clause. In 1990, Congress passed the Gun-Free School Zones Act, which made it a federal crime to possess a firearm on a school campus. Although schools operate under the direct supervision of the states, Congress justified the legislation using a broad reading of the Commerce Clause. When Alfonso Lopez was arrested for possessing a firearm on school grounds in San Antonio, Texas, federal prosecutors charged him with violating the Gun-Free School Zones Act. After his conviction in federal court, Lopez appealed on the basis that Congress had exceeded its regulatory powers under the Commerce Clause. In *United States v. Lopez* (1995), the Supreme Court struck down the Gun-Free School Zones Act as unconstitutional. The majority opinion, signed by five justices, ruled that Congress had exceeded its jurisdiction under the Commerce Clause by making the possession of a firearm on a school campus a federal crime.

While the *Lopez* decision halted the broadening of congressional powers under the Commerce Clause, it did not overturn any prior precedents, leaving in place the broad readings of the mid-twentieth century.

IMMIGRATION AND NATURALIZATION

Establishing Uniform Rules for American Citizenship

Across the globe, US citizenship is a coveted prize. Of the nine hundred million people worldwide who express a desire to immigrate to another country, nearly one in five claim the United States as their destination of choice, far exceeding any other country. US citizenship has many benefits, including visa-free travel to 188 foreign destinations and a high standard of living. While natural-born Americans receive the rights of citizenship by birth, those who aspire to become US citizens must follow a process in order to acquire it.

THE NATURALIZATION CLAUSE

The Naturalization Clause of the Constitution, found in Article I, Section 8, Clause 4, empowers Congress to "establish an uniform Rule of Naturalization." This gives Congress the power to establish laws to naturalize (grant citizenship to) individuals not born in the United States (or, in the early years of the republic, born to parents who were not US citizens). Under this clause, Americans are not only citizens of the states in which they reside; they are also citizens of the United States.

Although immigration is never mentioned in the Constitution, the Supreme Court has relied on the Naturalization Clause, in addition to the federal government's delegated constitutional authority to handle foreign relations, to rule that the federal government has exclusive authority under the Constitution to set immigration policy.

IMMIGRATION AND NATURALIZATION POLICY

Government policies concerning immigration and naturalization have evolved over the years through a combination of congressional legislation and Supreme Court decisions. This demonstrates both legislative and judicial influence on immigration and naturalization policy.

Naturalization Act of 1790

Congress first acted to create a uniform rule of naturalization with the Naturalization Act of 1790, which stated that "any alien, being a free white person, who shall have resided within the limits and under the jurisdiction of the United States for the term of two years" could become a citizen after demonstrating that they were "a person of good character" and swearing an oath to support the Constitution. Although the Constitution never links race with citizenship, Congress used its delegated naturalization power to make whiteness a prerequisite for citizenship. In spite of the racist nature of this particular provision, the 1790 act contains standards and procedures still in use today, such as requiring aspiring citizens to live in the United States for a period of time, to have a record free of any serious criminal activity, and to swear an oath to support the Constitution.

Naturalization Act of 1798

In 1798, the Federalist majority in Congress passed the Naturalization Act, which was part of the infamous package of legislation known as the Alien and Sedition Acts. The 1798 act raised the residency requirement to a staggering fourteen years (it had previously been five). The motivation for this unreasonable residency requirement was to stop recent immigrants, who were inclined to support Thomas Jefferson's Democratic-Republican Party, from gaining the right to vote. While the 1798 act did not violate the Constitution, it set an unfortunate precedent for political parties to use immigration and naturalization policy as a political tool.

Dred Scott v. Sandford

In addition to opening all federal territories to slavery, the infamous *Dred Scott v. Sandford* (1857) decision declared that people of African descent could not be US citizens. The *Dred Scott* decision was superseded by the Fourteenth Amendment, which guarantees birthright citizenship to all Americans without any regard to race.

Chinese Exclusion Act

In 1882, Congress passed the Chinese Exclusion Act in response to a public outcry against Chinese immigration to the United States. The Chinese Exclusion Act placed a ten-year ban on immigration from China (with a handful of exceptions), marking the first time that Congress used immigration policy to target a specific ethnic or national group.

Immigration Quota Acts

In the 1920s, Congress passed immigration quota acts that were designed to limit immigration from Southern and Eastern Europe. The quota acts of the 1920s sought to encourage immigration from Northern and Western Europe, whose populations were predominantly white, well educated, and Protestant, while placing limitations on immigration from other areas.

Immigration Act of 1965

The civil rights movement led Congress to reconsider immigration policies, which heavily favored white migrants. The Immigration and Nationality Act of 1965 eliminated these preferences while encouraging increased immigration from Africa, Asia, and the Middle East. The 1965 act also set a precedent for favoring applicants with specialized job skills, such as doctors and scientists.

Arizona v. United States

In *Arizona v. United States* (2012), the Supreme Court struck down an Arizona law that made it a state crime to be present in the state without legal federal documentation. The majority ruled that the states cannot make immigration policy, as it is a power delegated to Congress.

THE FUTURE OF IMMIGRATION AND NATURALIZATION POLICY

By making immigration and naturalization policy a federal power, the framers of the Constitution set the stage for the politicizing of this branch of policymaking. Presently, Democrats and Republicans are widely divided on immigration priorities. Although both political parties acknowledge the need for immigration reform, it is difficult to reconcile Democratic proposals for more generous pathways to citizenship with Republican proposals for stricter immigration controls and increased border security. It remains to be seen whether the current polarized climate will subside enough in the foreseeable future for Congress to take any decisive action regarding immigration and naturalization.

COINING MONEY AND PUNISHING COUNTERFEITING

Creating a Sound and Stable National Currency

A sound currency is essential to a sound economy. The framers sought to create a common market among the states through the Commerce Clause; however, this free trade required a stable and uniform currency to function properly. Under the Articles of Confederation, there was something of a currency crisis, as the states coined and printed their own money. State-controlled currency ended up being a hard economic lesson for the United States because it was impossible to weigh state currencies against each other or determine the value of federal currency compared to each state's currency. The lack of an easy monetary exchange created a commercial barrier among the states that stifled their potential for economic growth. The framers sought to remedy this issue by granting Congress the authority to coin money and punish counterfeiting.

COINAGE AND COUNTERFEITING CLAUSES

The Coinage and Counterfeiting Clauses of the Constitution are found in Article I, Section 8, Clauses 5 and 6. These clauses read as follows:

[The Congress shall have the power] To coin Money, regulate the Value thereof, and of foreign Coin, and fix the Standard of Weights and Measures; [and] To provide for the Punishment of counterfeiting the Securities and current Coin of the United States.

—Article I, Section 8, Clauses 5 and 6 of the Constitution

The Coining and Counterfeiting Clauses give Congress full control over the production of currency, which is reinforced by the prohibition on the states producing currency found in Article I, Section 10.

AN AVERSION TO PAPER MONEY

When the Constitution was written, monetary value was determined by the amount of hard (gold or silver) currency that backed its value. A piece of paper money was worthless if it could not be exchanged for precious metals. The framers worried about the tendency of both Congress and the states to print inflationary paper currency during the Confederation period. In 1787, Abigail Adams (wife of John Adams) wrote a letter to Thomas Jefferson, describing the chaos of Shays' Rebellion. She included the rebels' advocacy for paper currency as one of the direct causes of the rebellion.

By giving Congress the exclusive power to coin money (but not authorizing the printing of paper money), the framers hoped to halt the trend of printing paper money. It would be several decades before the federal government would print paper notes, beginning in 1861 with the issuing of paper "greenback" currency that was printed to finance the Civil War. While this was new at the time, Americans today use paper currency without thinking twice.

FEDERAL AGENCIES
INVOLVED IN CURRENCY

A number of federal agencies are involved in creating federal currency, determining its scarcity, and protecting its integrity. Each has a slightly different role in the federal process of managing currency.

- **The US Mint** produces all US coins circulated as legal tender. Today, coinage is minted in four locations: Philadelphia, Denver, San Francisco, and West Point. United States coinage includes a letter indicating where it is minted. Most common coins are minted at the Philadelphia and Denver mints, while the San Francisco and West Point mints tend to specialize in minting gold, silver, and commemorative coins.
- **The Bureau of Engraving and Printing**, located in Washington, DC, is responsible for the design and production (including printing) of all paper currency circulated in the United States.
- **The Federal Reserve System**, founded in 1913, is a central bank responsible for setting monetary policy, which includes determining the money supply. The Federal Reserve Board of Directors meets regularly to decide whether to expand or contract the money supply based on economic indicators, such as inflation.
- **The Secret Service** was created in 1865 to protect the integrity of US currency by investigating counterfeiting. Ironically, Abraham Lincoln signed the bill that created the Secret Service into law within a day of his assassination; however, the Secret Service did not become responsible for protecting the president until 1901 in the aftermath of the assassination of President William McKinley.

PUNISHING COUNTERFEITING

Penalties for counterfeiting in the United States are severe. Under Title 18, Section 471 of the US Code (a compendium of US laws), manufacturing or knowingly using counterfeit currency can result in up to twenty years in federal prison, in addition to heavy fines. The specific penalty depends on the gravity of the offense, such as the amount of counterfeit currency involved and the defendant's criminal history. It is also a federal offense to possess tools or materials designed for counterfeiting, including plates, blocks, dies, or digital equipment. Related offenses, such as fraud and forgery, can be penalized with significant prison time and fines. Courts may also order counterfeiters to pay restitution, particularly if there is identifiable financial harm to individuals, businesses, or financial institutions.

"White-Collar" Crime

Counterfeiting is an example of a "white-collar" crime, fitting into the category of nonviolent financially oriented crimes (such as tax evasion) that are often committed by white-collar professionals with upper-class backgrounds.

PENALTIES FOR PASSING COUNTERFEIT CURRENCY

Curiously, the federal government's exclusive delegated power of punishing counterfeiting does not extend to punishing attempts to pass counterfeit currency from one private party to another. In *Fox v. State of Ohio* (1847), the Supreme Court upheld the conviction of an Ohio woman who was found guilty of violating a state law against passing counterfeit currency. The Court distinguished between the act of creating counterfeit currency, in which one commits a direct offense against the federal government's power to create currency, and circulating counterfeit currency, which victimizes private parties. Attempting to knowingly pay for something with counterfeit currency is fraud, and most fraud cases are brought before state courts. Therefore, while the punishment of counterfeiters is delegated to the federal government, the federal and state governments share the concurrent power to punish those who circulate counterfeit currency.

WEIGHTS AND MEASURES

In addition to the power to coin money, Article I, Section 8, Clause 5 gives Congress the power to fix a standard set of weights and measures across the United States. The Constitution not only creates the conditions for a uniform currency; it also establishes a framework for goods exchanged across states to be measured in the same way, which also facilitates interstate commerce. While the exclusive power to coin money was new in the Constitution, the power to fix a standard for weights and measures is carried over from the Articles of Confederation.

The United States is one of only three countries, along with Liberia and Myanmar, that continues to officially use the old British imperial system of weights and measures (using feet, miles, gallons, and pints). Every other country in the world uses the metric system officially (although in Britain, the imperial system is used colloquially). Under the Constitution, only Congress has the power to change this system.

POST OFFICES AND POST ROADS

Distributing Mail Across the United States

Article I, Section 8, Clause 7 of the Constitution gives Congress the power "to establish Post Offices and post Roads." This simple line of text, known as the Postal Clause, grants Congress the power to regulate mail distribution across the United States and establish post offices. The Articles of Confederation gave Congress the same power. The Continental Congress established the first post office for the "United Colonies" in 1775, nearly a year before the Declaration of Independence, naming Benjamin Franklin as the first postmaster. However, today's US Postal Service developed largely after the ratification of the Constitution.

THE EARLY YEARS

The Americans who ratified the Constitution lived in a society without the mass-communication technologies that Americans today take for granted. There were no telephones, text messages, or emails. The only way to communicate with someone in another town or state was to send a letter. George Washington signed the Postal Service Act of 1792, which created a permanent postal service under the Constitution. The Postal Service Act allowed Americans to send private letters and also facilitated the spread of information, allowing for newspapers to be transported for far less than private letters. This helped Americans stay up to speed with the latest developments in other states.

Although Congress wasted little time in establishing a postal service, construction of post roads was limited in the early republic. Although the Constitution authorized Congress to construct post roads, states' rights advocates worried that this could lead to Congress exercising a general power to build roads. In 1806, Congress authorized the construction of the Cumberland Road, which connected Maryland to present-day West Virginia. This construction was useful for efficient mail delivery and enhanced interstate commerce. The Cumberland Road would eventually expand as far as Illinois, but limited federal funds and the advent of railroads led Congress to stop construction of this "National Road" after 1838. As a result, state roads served as the primary pathways of mail delivery in the early nineteenth century.

The Pony Express

The Pony Express, which carried mail from Missouri to California from 1860 to 1861, remains one of the most romanticized forms of mail delivery in the history of the United States, but it was not operated by the federal post office. During its brief existence, the Pony Express cut the time to get a message from the Eastern United States to California to only ten days. It shut its doors shortly after the first transcontinental telegraph line was completed in 1861.

Postage stamps are a vital part of the mail delivery process today, but Congress did not authorize federal postage stamps until 1847. Before this time, locally issued stamps were one of many ways to pay for postage, and recipients could choose to pay cash for postage upon delivery. The first stamps featured Benjamin Franklin and George Washington: the father of the post office and the father of the country. This began a long tradition of using postage stamps to celebrate important figures and events in American history. From Elvis Presley to Ella Baker, stamps have expressed America's diverse culture and history, one small square at a time.

TECHNOLOGICAL ADVANCEMENTS

The thundering trains of the American railroads revolutionized mail delivery in the United States. In 1869, the first transcontinental railroad linked the entire United States from Maine to California. The federal government contracted with railroad companies, which could carry mail much faster and more efficiently than horses could. This partnership with the railroads marked a significant leap in how quickly mail could be delivered (like upgrading from a bicycle to a sports car). It also set the stage for something even more revolutionary: the Railway Mail Service. This wasn't just about getting mail from point A to point B; it was a whole new way of sorting and handling mail, right there on the moving trains. It was a bit like having a mobile office zipping across the country, sorting letters and packages on the go, reaching their destinations with unprecedented speed and efficiency. In the twentieth century, the post office took to the skies, with airmail making its debut in 1918.

Transportation advancements were a giant leap in mail distribution, dramatically slashing the time it took for a letter or package to reach its destination. Alongside airmail, the twentieth century also saw the rise of motorized vehicles in mail delivery. Gone were the days of the horse-drawn carriage; now, sturdy trucks and vans zipped along roads, bringing mail to every nook and cranny of the nation. This shift to motorization wasn't just about speed; it also meant that the postal service could reach more people, even those in the most remote areas.

CONTEMPORARY DEBATES AND LEGAL CHALLENGES

In recent decades, the Postal Clause has become the center of several debates and legal challenges. First, there is the issue of monopoly and competition. Congress granted the postal service a monopoly on first-class mail, an arrangement that is justified under the Postal Clause. However, critics have called for deregulation and competition, which they believe could lead to faster service and lower prices. On the other hand, proponents argue that this monopoly is crucial to ensuring universal service and guaranteeing that every American, regardless of where they live, has access to reliable mail services. Concerns over the extent to which the government has the right to inspect private correspondence has sparked ongoing debate about where to draw the line between national security and individual privacy.

The Smithsonian National Postal Museum

Anyone interested in learning more about the historical role of the US Postal Service should consider a visit to the Smithsonian National Postal Museum in Washington, DC. Opened in 1993, the museum is known for its extensive collection of stamps and historical postal vehicles, including horse-drawn carriages and a full-sized railway mail car.

DECLARING WAR AND MAINTAINING THE MILITARY

Providing for the Common Defense

A key purpose of the Constitution is to provide for the common defense of the United States. Defending the nation is also listed as a justification for the taxing power found in Article I, Section 8, Clause 1. This federal power, like most other powers dealing with foreign relations, was carried over from the Articles of Confederation. A common defense was discussed as early as the French and Indian War, when Benjamin Franklin printed a cartoon featuring a snake cut up into several parts, with each part representing one of the thirteen colonies. The caption of Franklin's cartoon read "Join, or Die." The idea for a common defense was revisited at the start of the Revolutionary War in 1775, when the Second Continental Congress created the Continental Army, commanded by George Washington, to provide a defense for the thirteen colonies in their armed rebellion against the British.

CONGRESSIONAL AUTHORITY OVER THE ARMED FORCES

Article I, Section 8 of the Constitution includes several clauses that give Congress the power to declare war and maintain the army and navy. The enumerated powers of Congress regarding the military include: the power to declare war, to raise and support armies (appropriating money for their support for up to two years in advance), to provide for and maintain a navy, and to make rules governing the regulation of land and naval forces.

Each of these powers can be exercised by a concurrent majority of the Senate and the House of Representatives. The executive branch, however, holds the power to make peace treaties, empowering the president to negotiate treaties with the "advice and consent" of two-thirds of the Senate. While war cannot be declared without the consent of the House of Representatives, the House has no role in the peacemaking process. Once war is declared, the primary responsibility for conducting the war is passed to the president as commander in chief, with Congress having a check on the president through its power to appropriate (or withhold the appropriation of) funds for the war.

DECLARING WAR

Under the Constitution, Congress has declared war on five different occasions, with declarations of war against eleven countries. During the nineteenth century, Congress declared war against Great Britain in 1812, Mexico in 1846, and Spain in 1898. In the twentieth century, Congress has used its power to declare war only during the two world wars, with two separate declarations of war against Germany and Austria-Hungary during World War I and declarations against Japan, Germany, Italy, Bulgaria, Hungary, and Romania during World War II. Every other war fought in the history of the United States, including the Civil War, the Vietnam War, the Gulf War, and the Global War on Terror, have all been undeclared military conflicts in which the president was supported through congressional authorizations for the use of force.

The Hartford Convention

In the final days of the War of 1812, members of the Federalist Party from New England met in Hartford, Connecticut, to discuss amendments to the Constitution that would have curbed the war-making powers of Congress.

AN AVERSION TO STANDING ARMIES

Many of the Founding Fathers, including Thomas Jefferson, believed that peacetime standing armies were a threat to the liberty of a democratic republic. As the nation's third president, Jefferson signed the Military Peace Establishment Act in 1802, which made drastic reductions to the peacetime standing army of the United States. The same act provided for the establishment of a national military academy at West Point and the establishment of a Corps of Engineers. The United States would, for the most part, continue to maintain a minimal peacetime standing army through World War II, although the government invested heavily in the development of a powerful navy in the early years of the twentieth century. After World War II, the United States began maintaining a peacetime standing army in response to the communist threat during the Cold War with the Soviet Union between 1945 and 1991.

THE VIETNAM ERA

In the 1960s, Congress initially let the executive branch take the lead in directing the military action in South Vietnam. In the following decade, Congress sought to reassert its supervisory role. The Vietnam era is bookended by a pair of congressional resolutions.

The Gulf of Tonkin Resolution

During the Cold War, the United States was committed to containing the spread of communism in Europe, the Middle East, and Southeast Asia. In 1964, following an alleged attack by the communist North Vietnamese on the USS *Maddox*, Congress passed the Gulf of Tonkin Resolution, which gave President Lyndon Johnson a "blank check" to use force in the region. Within a few years, over half a million American military personnel were serving in Vietnam, resulting in an unpopular military draft that sparked student protests across university campuses nationwide. This resulted in a popular outcry to curb the president's power to use force overseas.

The War Powers Resolution

In 1973, Congress passed the War Powers Resolution. This joint resolution of Congress requires the president to notify Congress within forty-eight hours of deploying military forces overseas and receive congressional authorization for deployments exceeding sixty days. Sometimes called the War Powers Act, it actually carries no force of law as a joint resolution of Congress. While no president has formally acknowledged the validity of this resolution, presidents have generally operated within its parameters when deploying forces overseas.

The Future of the War-Making Power

Although it has been over eighty years since Congress declared war on any foreign country, the US military has operated in recent decades on every inhabited continent. It's uncertain whether Congress will ever use its power to declare war again or if authorizations for the use of military force have become the permanent new normal.

CALLING FORTH THE MILITIA

Bolstering National Defense with Citizen Soldiers

As dawn broke on the morning of April 19, 1775, a shot was fired in Lexington, Massachusetts. If Ralph Waldo Emerson is to be believed, that shot was heard "round the world." This shot was fired by a minuteman—one of many men in colonial Massachusetts who spent their days farming or working their trades while dedicating an occasional evening to military drills. They were civilians (not professional soldiers) committed to being ready in a figurative minute to join a paramilitary force in defense of their community in the case of an attack. As the Revolutionary War progressed, George Washington's professional Continental Army (and allied French forces) bore more of the burdens of battle, but it was militia forces who fired the first shots for American independence.

THE MILITIA CLAUSE

Article I, Section 8, Clause 15 of the Constitution gives Congress the power "to provide for calling forth the Militia to execute the Laws of the Union, suppress Insurrections and repel Invasions." When the Constitution was drafted, the Continental Army had been largely demobilized, as the Founders believed that a peacetime standing army was a frivolous expense and a threat to liberty—memories of occupying British troops were still fresh in the minds of Americans. They believed that professional armies were for times of war and that militia forces could ensure domestic tranquility and serve as the first line of defense during an invasion.

Although Congress has the power to enact guidelines for calling forth the militia, Article II of the Constitution designates the president as the commander in chief "of the Militia of the several States, when called into the actual Service of the United States." State militia units (referred to today as National Guard units) answer to the governor of each state unless they are mobilized for a specific purpose by the federal government.

THE WHISKEY REBELLION

The first test of the new federal government's ability to ensure domestic tranquility came in 1794. Farmers in western Pennsylvania organized an armed resistance to an excise tax on whiskey recently passed by Congress. At the time, these farmers distilled whiskey as a way to make additional money from their grain crops (and sometimes used it as currency when sound currency was scarce). These farmers believed that they were bearing more than their share of the weight of funding the federal government. When these tax protesters attacked the home of a federal tax collector, the federal government's authority was put to the test.

President Washington, who had been horrified by the chaos stirred up by Shays' Rebellion, responded to the national emergency with urgency. He requested militia forces from the governors of Pennsylvania and the neighboring states of Virginia, Maryland, and New Jersey, assembling an overwhelming force of around thirteen thousand men in response to the rebellious force of around five hundred. By the time the federal militia arrived in western Pennsylvania, the rebels seemed to have received the message and dispersed. As Thomas Jefferson put it in a private letter, "an insurrection was announced and proclaimed and armed against, and marched against, but could never be found." The federal government had demonstrated its ability to ensure domestic tranquility in the face of insurrectionary violence against its authority.

THE COMMANDER IN CHIEF

Although nothing in the Constitution denies the president the authority to exercise direct battlefield command of the military, no president has ever done so. There is a common misconception that Washington took command of the militia force raised against the Whiskey Rebellion, but he actually inspected the militia before handing over command to his fellow Virginian Henry "Light-Horse Harry" Lee (father of the future Confederate general, Robert E. Lee).

THE CIVIL WAR

In 1861, President Lincoln called forth the militia, asking state governors to provide him with a force of seventy-five thousand men after Confederates fired on Fort Sumter. The situation was much different than the Whiskey Rebellion. The forces that attacked Sumter were acting on the orders of their recently seceded state governments. Confederate leaders claimed that states had the right to secede under the Tenth Amendment (since the Constitution never expressly prohibits states from seceding). However, Lincoln insisted that the idea of secession was unconstitutional, running counter to the idea of a "More Perfect Union."

Whereas the laws of the United States have been opposed...by combinations too powerful to be suppressed by the ordinary course of judicial proceedings...I Abraham Lincoln President of the United States, in virtue of the power in me vested by the Constitution...hereby do call forth the militia of the several states...to cause the laws to be duly executed.

—Lincoln's Proclamation on State Militia

The Civil War, in which over six hundred thousand Americans were killed, began with the calling forth of state militia forces on April 15, 1861, to put down what was deemed at the time to be a mere insurrectionary disturbance.

MILITIAS IN CONTEMPORARY AMERICA

More recently, the militia clause has been occasionally invoked in response to civil disturbances and natural disasters. During the civil rights movement, President Kennedy mobilized the Alabama National Guard to assist with desegregating the University of Alabama when the state's governor refused to cooperate with federal court orders. In recent wars in Vietnam, Afghanistan, and Iraq, presidents have used the militia clause to send National Guard units overseas to support regular military units in the field. However, Americans today are most likely to see National Guard units acting in their standard capacities, providing logistical support during natural disasters and emergencies under the direction of state governors.

NECESSARY AND PROPER

Interpreting the Constitution's "Elastic Clause"

Article I, Section 8 of the US Constitution enumerates the powers delegated to Congress, such as collecting taxes and regulating interstate commerce. Congress is supposed to operate within the limits of these powers. However, the framers wanted this new government to be able to pass the legislation that would be necessary for executing all of its powers and responsibilities. For this reason, the framers concluded Article I, Section 8 with the Necessary and Proper Clause (also known as the Elastic Clause).

> The Congress shall have Power...To make all Laws which shall be necessary and proper for carrying into Execution the foregoing Powers, and all other Powers vested by this Constitution in the Government of the United States, or in any Department or Officer thereof.
>
> —The Necessary and Proper Clause,
> Article I, Section 8 of the Constitution

Antifederalists opposed the Necessary and Proper Clause, worried that the federal government could make up a justification to pass any legislation whatsoever. In Federalist No. 33, Alexander Hamilton accused the Antifederalists' opponents of misrepresenting the clause and exaggerating its potential for abuse. Hamilton insisted that the Necessary and Proper Clause would only enable Congress to pass laws related to the enumerated powers. Plus, this clause would protect the federal government from efforts by the states to obstruct constitutional legislation. While the Constitution was ultimately ratified with the Necessary and Proper Clause intact, the debate over the clause's meaning was only beginning.

THE NATIONAL BANK

After George Washington was unanimously elected as president, he assembled a small cabinet of experienced leaders to advise and help him administer the departments within the executive branch. Washington's first cabinet included Thomas Jefferson as secretary of state and Alexander Hamilton as secretary of the treasury. Hamilton had a number of ambitious plans to improve public credit and promote economic development. The most controversial of these proposals was his plan to charter a national bank. Hamilton argued that the national bank was constitutional because it would facilitate the federal government's exercise of its financially oriented enumerated powers. The bank could lend money to the federal government, provide a secure place for depositing tax revenues, and create a uniform currency. Although it seemed like a good idea, there was a problem: The Constitution doesn't authorize a national bank.

Critics claimed that Hamilton's proposed bank was unconstitutional on the basis of the Necessary and Proper Clause. Jefferson and Attorney General Edmund Randolph argued that the establishment of a national bank was unconstitutional because the Constitution does not mention the creation of a bank (or any for-profit corporation). Additionally, Jefferson argued that since every enumerated power could be executed without chartering a national bank, the bank was not "necessary" for the government to perform its core functions.

It has been much urged that a bank will give great facility, or convenience in the collection of taxes. Suppose this were true: yet the Constitution allows only the means which are "necessary" not those which are merely "convenient" for effecting the enumerated powers.

—Thomas Jefferson to George Washington

Jefferson's conclusions about the national bank were driven by his belief in strict constructionism, which aims to interpret the Constitution exactly as it is written. Strict constructionists view the Constitution as a limited grant of power to the federal government, and they believe only a constitutional amendment can grant additional powers. A strict constructionist would interpret the Necessary and Proper Clause to apply only to legislation that is absolutely necessary to carry out its primary responsibilities. Alexander Hamilton, however, advocated for loose constructionism, which argues for the existence of implied powers in addition to the enumerated powers.

Every power vested in a government is in its nature sovereign, and includes, by force of the term, a right to employ all the means requisite...and which are not precluded by restrictions and exceptions specified in the Constitution, or not immoral, or not contrary to the essential ends of political society.

—Alexander Hamilton to George Washington

In Hamilton's view, the enumeration of financial powers, such as the power to tax and coin money, implied the power to create a financial institution that would make it easier for the federal government to exercise these powers. Hamilton also took issue with Jefferson's stringent interpretation of the word *necessary*, noting that the word is often used to reference something useful. For example, someone might say it's necessary to have a fork in order to eat spaghetti, but a pair of chopsticks might do in a pinch.

President Washington signed the bank bill into law, persuaded by Hamilton's loose constructionism. Congress allowed the First Bank of the United States to expire after its initial twenty-year charter ended in 1811, but after the War of 1812, President James Madison signed a bill creating the Second Bank of the United States in 1816. In the 1790s, Madison had joined Jefferson in denouncing a national bank as unconstitutional, but the debt accumulated during the second war with Britain convinced him that a national bank had become "necessary and proper" to pay war debt and establish a stable currency. The Supreme Court officially upheld the constitutionality of the national bank (and the loose-constructionist doctrine of implied powers) in its *McCulloch v. Maryland* decision, which will be discussed later.

RECENT JURISPRUDENCE

To this date, the Supreme Court has never struck down a federal law on the basis of it failing to meet the Constitution's standard of "necessary." There was one case, however, in which the Court ruled that a federal law was not "proper" in its execution. Under the leadership of Chief Justice William Rehnquist, who led the Supreme Court from 1986 to 2005, the Court's majority embraced the judicial philosophy of New Federalism, which tended to defer to the states in disputes over constitutional gray areas.

In 1993, Congress passed the Brady Handgun Violence Prevention Act (more commonly known as the "Brady Bill"), which established a federal background check system for handgun purchasers. The law stated that during the interval between the passage of the law and the implementation of a background check system, state and local law enforcement officers would be responsible for carrying out the background checks on behalf of the federal government. In a 5–4 decision, the Court's conservative majority ruled in *Printz v. United States* (1997) that it was not "proper" for Congress to require state officials to carry out federal background checks. Although the whole matter was rendered moot by the FBI's launch of the National Instant Criminal Background Check System in 1998, the *Printz* decision shows that the interpretation of the Necessary and Proper Clause is still open to debate.

POWERS DENIED TO CONGRESS

Limiting the Powers of the Federal Legislature

Much of Article I of the Constitution focuses on organizing the legislative branch of the federal government and delegating several enumerated and implied powers to Congress. While Article I, Section 8 delegates powers to Congress, Article I, Section 9 pivots to another of the Constitution's core functions: the limitation of the government's powers.

LIMITING CONGRESSIONAL POWER

Article I, Section 9 contains several prohibitions to keep Congress from taking specific actions that are incompatible with the idea of a constitutional federal republic. By clearly listing specific limitations on the powers of Congress, Section 9 foreshadows additional restrictions on Congress that are found in the Bill of Rights.

Regulation of the International Slave Trade

The original Constitution forbade Congress from passing any legislation prohibiting the "Migration or Importation of such Persons as any of the States now existing shall think proper to admit" for twenty years. This clause was a compromise between delegates from free states, who wanted to give Congress the power to end the international slave trade, and delegates from slave states, who were still importing enslaved people. The language of this clause reflected the framers' resolve not to mention slavery or the slave trade directly in the Constitution. Congress passed an act ending the international slave trade in 1808—the first year Congress could legally do so.

Suspension of Habeas Corpus

The Suspension Clause of the Constitution forbids federal authorities from denying a writ of habeas corpus to anyone who has been arrested and held by the government. Habeas corpus limits the amount of time that someone can be detained without being charged with a crime. Americans, then, cannot be indefinitely detained without being formally charged with a crime and scheduled for trial. Depending on the jurisdiction, the maximum amount of time that an individual can be held without being charged is forty-eight or seventy-two hours.

The protection of habeas corpus is regarded as a "privilege" under the Constitution rather than an absolute right. Although the Constitution forbids the government from suspending habeas corpus in normal circumstances, it makes an exception "in Cases of Rebellion or Invasion the public Safety may require it." During the American Civil War, President Lincoln, with the support of Congress, suspended writs of habeas corpus several times. These suspensions did not violate the Constitution because they occurred when rebellion placed the safety of the nation at risk.

Bills of Attainder

In the English legal tradition, Parliament had the authority to pass bills of attainder, which declared a person guilty of criminal activity by a legislative vote. After the passage of a bill of attainder, the "attainted" person's life was considered forfeit and outside of the protection of the law. As such, anyone who saw the person could kill them on sight without facing any legal repercussions. Generally, bills of attainder were passed against people who were obviously guilty of treasonous actions, but they could also be used against people who were unpopular with Parliament. A bill of attainder provided authorities with a convenient alternative to a judicial trial, in which an accused person's guilt must be established "beyond a reasonable doubt" based on the evidence presented against them.

The Constitution forbids Congress to pass bills of attainder, as such bills deprive accused persons of due process of law. Also, by circumventing standard trial procedure, a legislature passing a bill of attainder directly exercises judicial powers, violating the constitutional principle of separation of powers.

Ex Post Facto Laws

Under the Constitution, Congress is not allowed to pass ex post facto (after the fact) laws that would take effect retroactively. An American can only be found guilty of violating a criminal statute if the crime was committed after a law took effect. Furthermore, someone convicted of a crime must be punished based on the criminal penalties that were in force when the crime was committed.

Taxes on Exports

Congress has the authority to collect tariffs on imported goods to fund the government, but the Constitution prohibits the taxation of exports. Since it is standard practice for nations to place tariffs on imported goods, this provision of the Constitution protects exporters from having to pay a tax on the same goods twice during the export process. Furthermore, the prevailing economic theories of the time emphasized the importance of a favorable balance of trade, in which exports exceed imports.

Budgetary Transparency

Congress is required by the Constitution to spend money only as properly appropriated by law and to publicly publish all of its tax receipts and expenditures on a regular basis. Americans can freely access annual reports that detail the specific sources of federal revenue and the budgets of each federal department. In a democratic republic, the people deserve an accounting of how public funds are raised and spent.

Titles of Nobility and Foreign Emoluments

The Constitution forbids Congress from granting anyone a title of nobility. Such titles are a hallmark of monarchies, which have fixed social hierarchies and distinctions between commoners and nobles. Titles of nobility are an affront to the very nature of republican government, in which the idea of monarchy is rejected and all citizens are equal under the law. Furthermore, individuals who hold government positions are barred from "accept[ing] of any present, Emolument, Office, or Title, of any kind whatever, from any King, Prince, or foreign State" without the consent of Congress. The Foreign Emoluments Clause was designed to shield the US government from foreign influence, which had spurred the downfall of many historical republics, as Hamilton pointed out in Federalist No. 22. If government officials cannot accept large gifts from foreign dignitaries, they have less incentive to place their loyalties with anyone from outside of the United States.

Sir Norman?

In 1991, Queen Elizabeth II bestowed an honorary knighthood on US Army General Norman Schwarzkopf, who commanded American and British forces in Operation Desert Storm. Although "Stormin' Norman" was an active US Army officer at the time, the honor did not create a constitutional crisis. Since Schwarzkopf was not a British subject, he did not kneel before the queen during the ceremony, and the honorary knighthood did not confer a title of nobility.

POWERS DENIED TO THE STATES

Clarifying the Limits of Federalism

A federal constitution must limit the powers of the state governments to keep them from interfering with the federal government's exercise of its delegated powers. While there are some powers in the Constitution that the states and federal government exercise concurrently, there are also delegated powers that are only to be exercised by the federal government, as well as others that are not to be exercised by *any* government operating under the Constitution. Article I, Section 10 of the Constitution focuses specifically on prohibiting the states from exercising certain powers within the federal system. These prohibitions are outlined in three clauses.

POWERS ALWAYS DENIED TO THE STATES

The first clause of Article I, Section 10 lists powers that no state shall exercise under any circumstances under the Constitution.

> No State shall enter into any Treaty, Alliance, or Confederation; grant Letters of Marque and Reprisal; coin Money; emit Bills of Credit; make any Thing but gold and silver Coin a Tender in Payment of Debts; pass any Bill of Attainder, ex post facto Law, or Law impairing the Obligation of Contracts, or grant any Title of Nobility.
>
> —Article I, Section 10, Clause 1 of the Constitution

Among the powers forbidden to the states in Clause 1 are powers that are also forbidden to Congress because of their antirepublican character, such as bills of attainder, ex post facto laws, and titles of nobility. In addition, the states are prohibited from conducting foreign relations by entering into treaties, alliances, and confederations outside of the Constitution.

Letters of Marque and Reprisal

At the time of the Constitutional Convention, it was a common practice for wartime governments to commission the owners of privately owned ships as privateers. Letters of marque and reprisal gave privateers legal sanction to raid enemy commerce. The Constitution expressly forbids the states from exercising this archaic war-making power.

Protecting Currency and Contracts

The Constitution limits the ability of state legislatures (where populist politicians often tried to win the favor of the people by canceling debts and printing paper money) to undermine sound currency and financial contracts. The Constitution does not allow states to pass legislation that is designed to undermine financial contracts or cancel legitimate debts. The states are also prohibited from coining their own money or printing "bills of credit" in the form of paper money not backed by precious metals. Additionally, the states may not recognize anything other than gold and silver as legal tender for the payment of debts. Recently, several states, including Utah and Louisiana, passed legislation making gold and silver coins produced by the US Mint legal tender within their jurisdictions.

PROHIBITION ON TAXING TRADE

Article I, Section 10, Clause 2 of the Constitution forbids states from taxing any imports or exports without the express consent of Congress. This provision of the Constitution firmly establishes the taxation of imports as a delegated power of Congress, and neither the federal nor state governments may tax exports.

PROHIBITIONS ON MAINTAINING MILITARY FORCES

Article I, Section 10, Clause 3 of the Constitution prohibits the states from maintaining troops and warships in times of peace. Although states do not raise armies during wartime today, the federal government used to rely on states to raise military units during wartime, including during the American Civil War. States are also prohibited from engaging in war "unless actually invaded, or in such imminent Danger as will not admit of delay." In 1838, Maine authorized funds for raising military forces during a brief border dispute with the British colony of New Brunswick (today part of Canada) known as the Aroostook War. Maine's authorities justified the appropriation on the grounds that the British had invaded their state. In 1842, the Webster-Ashburton Treaty resolved the border dispute and ended the undeclared war before the two sides ever confronted each other on a battlefield.

Chapter 4

The Executive Branch

The legislative branch is the most foundational to a democratic republic (where the people elect representatives to make laws on their behalf), but the executive branch is the most immediately visible and impactful to the lives of everyday Americans. As a separate branch of government that is equal with the legislative, the executive branch operates within the boundaries of the law, though with a great deal of independence and discretion. Unlike parliamentary systems of government, in which the laws are executed by leaders of the legislative body, the framers placed the execution of the laws in the hands of a president.

The president of the United States is by far the most visible leader of the federal government. In the late twentieth century, the president was often referred to as the "leader of the free world." As the sole director of the executive branch of the federal government, the president must wear many hats, including that of chief executive, commander in chief, and chief diplomat. Article II of the Constitution details the many powers and responsibilities of the president and the executive branch.

THE EXECUTIVE POWER

The Creation of the American Presidency

The US Constitution creates an independent executive branch that is separate from the legislative and judicial branches. While the legislative branch has the power to make laws, and the judicial branch has the power to resolve disputes concerning the laws, the executive branch has the exclusive authority to enforce the laws and carry out the day-to-day operations of the government. The Articles of Confederation made no provision for an independent executive branch, and although Congress made a provision for a Council of the States in 1784, this body never effectively met or transacted any business, leaving federal laws largely unenforced. Even if the Council of the States had met, it would not have been independent in any way but would have been subject to the control of Congress and the states.

THE EXECUTIVE POWER

In the first clause of Article II of the Constitution, the framers placed executive authority in the hands of a single individual, known as the president.

> The executive Power shall be vested in a President of the United States of America.
>
> —Article II, Section 1, Clause 1 of the Constitution

In their creation of a president who would exercise executive authority independently from the legislative branch, the framers were inspired by the writings of Montesquieu, a political theorist of the French Enlightenment whose best-known work, *The Spirit of the Laws*, was an instant classic in political philosophy. Montesquieu identified four dimensions of executive power: making peace and war, sending and receiving embassies, protecting against invasions, and establishing public security.

Making Peace and War

While the Constitution gives Congress the sole power to declare war, the president is named as the commander in chief of the armed forces, giving the president exclusive authority to direct military forces during wartime (although Congress can check the president's power by refusing to appropriate money for the armed forces). Although Congress takes the lead in declaring war, the president leads in making peace, possessing the authority to negotiate treaties with the advice and consent of the Senate.

Sending and Receiving Embassies

The president functions as the "chief diplomat" of the United States. The Constitution gives the president the authority (again, with the advice and consent of the Senate) to appoint ambassadors to represent the United States in foreign countries, as well as to receive foreign ambassadors representing the interests of their governments in the United States. By giving the president the power to receive ambassadors, the Constitution designates the president as the ceremonial head of state, a function that is traditionally exercised by the ruler in monarchical systems of government.

The Head of State

Since the Constitution creates three coequal branches of government, the United States does not have a head of government, which is a function exercised by a prime minister in monarchies and parliamentary democracies. However, the president serves as the head of state, functioning as an overall figurehead for the United States in its relations with other countries.

Protecting Against Invasions

Part of the president's responsibility as commander in chief is to protect the United States from foreign invasions. Even in times of peace, the president is responsible for making sure that the armed forces maintain a degree of readiness that will discourage would-be enemies from attacking. "We know only too well that war comes not when the forces of freedom are strong, but when they are weak," then-candidate Ronald Reagan said when accepting the Republican Party's nomination to the presidency in 1980. Reagan's "Peace Through Strength" plan is one of many examples of presidents taking responsibility for military readiness even in times of peace.

Establishing Public Security

In addition to the powers over foreign relations, the president's position as chief executive carries the responsibility for enforcing federal laws, guaranteeing that the rule of law remains established so that citizens feel safe and free to pursue their happiness. The president is in charge of organizing federal departments and has the authority to appoint the leaders of federal law enforcement agencies, such as the FBI.

AN INDEPENDENT BRANCH

American presidents are elected by a process that excludes both Congress and the Supreme Court, and they exercise many of their powers independently from the direction of the other branches. Conversely, the president has no authority to legislate or judge disputes between parties in the courts. This is exactly what the framers intended, following the direction of Montesquieu. In *The Spirit of the Laws*, Montesquieu argued that an independent executive branch of government is essential to the maintenance of a free society.

> When the legislative and executive powers are united in the same person, or in the same body of magistrates, there can be no liberty....There would be an end of everything, were the same man...to exercise [legislative, executive, and judicial] powers.
> —*The Spirit of the Laws*, Book XI, Chapter 6

In giving the president executive power while giving legislative and judicial powers to other branches, the framers sought to give the president independent power within reasonable limits.

A UNITARY EXECUTIVE

In addition to creating an independent executive branch, the framers of the Constitution chose to place this branch in the hands of a unitary executive. This decision was reached after extensive debate. The convention considered the proposal for a unitary executive from James Wilson, a delegate from Pennsylvania, and the proposal for a three-person executive committee advanced by Edmund Randolph, a delegate from Virginia. Randolph's argument that a unitary executive was reminiscent of monarchy resonated with those who believed that the Constitution should adhere to the principles of a republican form of government. However, Wilson argued that placing the executive functions in the hands of a three-person committee would lead to needless interruptions in the administration of the government due to personal rivalries between committee members.

Elbridge Gerry, a delegate from Massachusetts, compared Randolph's plan for a three-person committee to "a general with three heads" that would be especially harmful in exercising authority over the military. Persuaded by the pragmatism of Wilson's plan, the convention voted in favor of the proposal for a unitary executive by a vote of seven states to three.

A PRESIDENTIAL REPUBLIC

The Constitution created the first presidential republic in the modern world. Since then, presidential republics, in which the leader of the executive branch operates with complete independence from the legislature, have spread worldwide (with particular predominance in the Americas). Not every nation that has a president has a presidential system, however. Some nations, such as Israel and Pakistan, have presidents who are chosen by the legislative branch to exercise the ceremonial functions of a head of state while holding little to no executive power.

ANTIFEDERALIST OPPOSITION

Just as some of the delegates at the Constitutional Convention had expressed doubts about a unitary executive, Antifederalists chose the presidency as one of their favorite targets in their arguments against ratification. "Wherein does this president, invested with his powers and prerogatives, essentially differ from the king of Great Britain?" asked an Antifederalist from New York (likely the state's governor) bearing the pseudonym of "Cato."

HAMILTON'S DEFENSE OF A UNITARY EXECUTIVE

Alexander Hamilton countered Antifederalist attacks on the unitary executive in *The Federalist Papers*. He argued that a unitary executive was essential for the government to have the necessary energy for the vigorous enforcement of the laws.

> Energy in the Executive is a leading character in the definition of good government. It is essential to the protection of the community against foreign attacks...to the steady administration of the laws [and] to the protection of property.
>
> —Federalist No. 70 (Hamilton)

In the end, Hamilton's pragmatic arguments in favor of an energetic executive proved more persuasive than those of the Antifederalists, who stirred up fears of monarchy without proposing a viable alternative that could get the job done just as efficiently.

EXECUTIVE DEPARTMENTS

The Cabinet and Federal Agencies

The Constitution puts the president in charge of the operations of the entire executive branch of the US government. This would be a daunting task for any individual to tackle. Fortunately, the Constitution provides plenty of help for the president. As the chief executive, it is the president's responsibility to select people to run the many departments that make up the executive branch.

THE EXECUTIVE DEPARTMENTS

The Constitution gives the president broad powers to appoint a number of executive branch officials, including the heads of every executive department, with the advice and consent of the Senate.

> He...by and with the Advice and Consent of the Senate, shall appoint Ambassadors, other public Ministers and Consuls...and all other Officers of the United States, whose Appointments are not herein otherwise provided for, and which shall be established by Law: but the Congress may by Law vest the Appointment of such inferior Officers, as they think proper, in the President alone, in the Courts of Law, or in the Heads of Departments.
>
> —Article II, Section 2, Clause 2 of the Constitution

The Constitution does not specify which federal departments will be created, leaving this to the discretion of Congress. Over the years, Congress has created a number of executive departments, which include the Department of State and the Department of Defense, which handle foreign relations and the military, respectively, on the president's behalf. While the Departments of State and Defense perform delegated functions of the federal government that are not shared with the states, more recently created federal departments, such as the Department of Education, cooperate with state agencies in areas where the Constitution reserves direct control to the states.

THE PRESIDENT'S CABINET

The president's cabinet is a group that advises the president. Although the Constitution never specifically mentions that the president will have a cabinet, it does state that the president may ask executive branch officials for advice from time to time.

> The President...may require the Opinion, in writing, of the principal Officer in each of the executive Departments, upon any Subject relating to the Duties of their respective Offices.
>
> —Article II, Section 2, Clause 1 of the Constitution

The officers who run the executive departments do not run their departments independently but are directly answerable to the president. The idea of a cabinet began to take shape during George Washington's presidency, when he found it more expedient for his department heads to come together and discuss matters of importance in person. Although this may sound like the kind of executive committee that the framers rejected at the Constitutional Convention, the cabinet is not a body with any legal authority, and the president maintains sole authority to make decisions (even if it means rejecting the advice of the cabinet).

President Washington's cabinet included only four people: Secretary of State Thomas Jefferson, Secretary of the Treasury Alexander Hamilton, Secretary of War Henry Knox, and Attorney General Edmund Randolph. Interestingly, the original cabinet did not include Vice President John Adams, who Washington believed had a conflict of interest due to his role in the legislative branch as president of the Senate. However, it became a standard practice in the twentieth century for presidents to include their vice presidents in the cabinet and rely on them for advice. In contrast to Washington's small cabinet, President Joe Biden assembled a cabinet that included the vice president and twenty-five other federal officials.

The "Kitchen Cabinet"

Many presidents have chosen to confide in close friends, assembling informal "kitchen cabinets" to advise them on big decisions. This term was first used during the presidency of Andrew Jackson, whose troublesome relationship with his official cabinet was well known. Ronald Reagan often consulted with his "kitchen cabinet" of California businessmen.

Since the cabinet is an informal body, each president decides which executive offices are cabinet-level positions. Some executive positions, such as the US ambassador to the United Nations, move in and out of the cabinet. President Dwight D. Eisenhower raised the position of UN ambassador to cabinet-level rank after appointing his political ally Henry Cabot Lodge Jr. to the position. Since the presidency of George H. W. Bush, the UN ambassador has been downgraded from and restored to cabinet status at the discretion of individual presidents. A UN ambassador with cabinet status reports directly to the president, while an ambassador without cabinet status reports directly to the secretary of state.

AT THE PLEASURE OF THE PRESIDENT

Although the Constitution requires cabinet members and senior officials in the executive departments to be confirmed by the Senate, they serve "at the pleasure of" the president after they are confirmed. This means that the president can fire cabinet members and senior officials for any reason (or for no reason) without needing anyone's approval. The Supreme Court held in *Myers v. United States* (1926) that the Senate cannot limit the president's removal powers because the Constitution doesn't give the Senate this power. If the Senate had the power to stop the president from firing executive officials, it would throw off the system of checks and balances. A federal official with enough friends in the Senate, for example, could defy the president without facing any consequences. If that were to happen, the president would cease to be in control of the executive branch.

CIVIL SERVICE REFORM

For over a century after the Constitution was ratified, presidents had the sole authority to appoint or remove every employee in the executive branch of government. While early presidents used this power in moderation, Andrew Jackson replaced every employee in the executive branch (even local postmasters) with someone who was loyal to him. This began the "spoils system," which was abused by presidents for decades to reward political loyalists.

In the decades after the Civil War, there was an outcry for reforms that would reduce corruption in the federal government. In 1883, Congress passed the Pendleton Civil Service Act, which insulated most employees in the executive branch from arbitrary removal by the president. While the president maintains appointment and removal powers of senior officials in the executive branch, most federal employees are career professionals who maintain their jobs regardless of which president or party is in office.

INDEPENDENT AGENCIES

The executive branch also includes several independent agencies, which are governed by boards appointed by the president with the advice and consent of the Senate. Unlike the standard executive departments, whose senior officials serve at the pleasure of the president, the boards of independent agencies function outside of the president's direct control, and the president must demonstrate cause prior to removing a person from the board of an independent agency.

The first independent agency to be created by Congress was the Interstate Commerce Commission, which was created in 1887 in order to regulate the railroads. Congress placed the commission outside of the direct control of the president in order to reduce corruption and political influence. During the twentieth century, Congress created several more independent agencies, including the Federal Election Commission, the Federal Reserve System, and the Securities and Exchange Commission.

THE COMMANDER IN CHIEF
Presidential Control of the Military

One of the most important functions of the federal government under the Constitution is providing for the common defense. This delegated power, carried over from the Articles of Confederation, was the most important reason that the newly independent states came together to form a common government. As mentioned earlier, making war and protecting the country from invasion are two of the most important components of the executive branch of government. In addition to directing the administration of the executive departments as chief executive, the president also directs the military as commander in chief of the armed forces.

THE COMMANDER IN CHIEF

The President shall be Commander in Chief of the Army and Navy of the United States, and of the Militia of the several States, when called into the actual Service of the United States.
—Article II, Section 2, Clause 1 of the Constitution

As commander in chief of the armed forces, the president exercises complete authority over all US military forces as well as state militia (National Guard) units when they are called to serve in a federal capacity. When the Constitution was ratified, this power was typically held by European monarchs (usually in a ceremonial capacity).

CIVILIAN CONTROL OF THE MILITARY

The president's role as commander in chief reflects the importance of civilian control of the military in a democratic republic. Since the government's power comes from the people, the people's elected representatives should have the final say in matters of peace and war. As Georges Clemenceau, who served as prime minister of France during World War I, said: "War is too important to be left to the generals." Civilian control of the military is sometimes compromised, such as when Napoleon overthrew the civilian government of France in a military coup in 1799. In today's world, military coups still happen in developing countries without strong democratic institutions. However, in establishing civilian control of the military, the Constitution has created a government in which the people have ruled through their elected representatives for over 230 years without a single period of military rule.

MILITARY SERVICE OF PRESIDENTS

Although the Constitution designates the president as commander in chief of the armed forces, there is no constitutional requirement that the president have any military experience. Of the forty-five men who have served as president, thirty-one served in the military prior to their presidencies. Of those thirty-one who served, twelve attained the rank of general officer. The presidents who reached the highest levels of the military command structure were George Washington, Ulysses S. Grant, and Dwight D. Eisenhower, each of whom exercised overall command of military forces in the wars prior to their elections. Neither Washington, Grant, nor Eisenhower had ever served in an elected office prior to being elected president.

Although two out of three presidents served in the military before becoming president, military service as a road to the presidency is less common in the twenty-first century. The last president to have any record of military service was George W. Bush, who served in the Texas and Alabama Air National Guards, and the last president with any combat experience was his father, George H. W. Bush. Since the United States has had an all-volunteer military since 1972, the current percentage of Americans who have served in the military is lower in comparison to the decades following the Civil War, the world wars, and the Vietnam War. With this in mind, it may be some time before Americans elect another president with military service.

General of the Armies

In 1976, Congress voted to posthumously elevate George Washington to the rank of General of the Armies, a "six-star" rank that had only been held by John J. Pershing, who commanded the American Expeditionary Forces during World War I. Elevating Washington's rank to that of Pershing's ensured that the father of our country would not be outranked by any other military officer.

ROLE IN DECLARING WAR

Although the Constitution gives Congress the sole authority to declare war, James Madison set a precedent for the president's initiation of this process when he sent a letter to Congress asking for a declaration of war against Britain in 1812. This letter became popularly known as Madison's "War Message." Presidents Polk, McKinley, Wilson, and Franklin D. Roosevelt all followed Madison's precedent in requesting declarations of war against Mexico, Spain,

Germany, and Japan, respectively. Wilson, the first president in over a century to deliver the State of the Union address in person, delivered his war message as a speech rather than in writing. Roosevelt's war message, which declared December 7 as "a date which will live in infamy," made a permanent impression on the American mind.

CONGRESSIONAL CHECKS ON THE PRESIDENT'S POWERS

Although the president exercises overall command of the armed forces, Congress has some checks on the president's military powers. The president cannot appropriate money for the armed forces, so Congress can inhibit the president's authority by using the "power of the purse." Congress can also take action to limit where the military can operate. During the Vietnam War, Congress pushed back against the Nixon administration's incursions into Cambodia, where Congress had never authorized the president to use military force. While the president can initiate limited military actions without consulting Congress (one of the most recent being missile strikes against Houthi terrorists in Yemen who were firing on cargo ships in the Red Sea), Congress maintains its right through the War Powers Resolution of 1973 to authorize any military action exceeding sixty days.

MEMORABLE MOMENTS

Presidents have occasionally used their powers as commander in chief in creative ways. In 1863, Abraham Lincoln used his power as commander in chief to direct the Union Army to free enslaved people in Confederate-held territories. By framing the Emancipation Proclamation as a "necessary war measure," he argued that the proclamation was a constitutional use of his powers as commander in chief (he advocated aggressively for the Thirteenth Amendment partly out of a concern that his Emancipation Proclamation might be overturned in the courts). In 1907, Theodore Roosevelt ordered a naval force known as the Great White Fleet to circumnavigate the globe in a voyage that had no other direct purpose than to show off American naval power across the globe. The voyage of the Great White Fleet demonstrated that the president's power as commander in chief extends even into the sphere of public relations.

THE POWER TO PARDON

The President's Uncheckable Power to Forgive

The Constitution sets up a very intricate system of checks and balances. For example, the president's veto power is not absolute, as Congress can override a veto by a two-thirds vote of both houses. The president's power as commander in chief is balanced by congressional authority to declare war and make military appropriations. However, there is one presidential power in the Constitution that stands out like a sore thumb from the others due to an inability of the other branches to check it: the power to pardon.

THE PRESIDENT'S PARDONING POWER

> The President...shall have Power to grant Reprieves and Pardons for Offences against the United States, except in Cases of Impeachment.
> —Article II, Section 2, Clause 1 of the Constitution

In simple language, this means that the president has the power to forgive anyone who has either been accused or found guilty of a federal crime. The pardoning power can take the form of pardons, reprieves, commutations, and amnesties.

Pardons

A presidential pardon forgives the recipient for breaking a federal law and exempts them from further prosecution or punishment for the crime. Although the person receiving a pardon escapes further prosecution and punishment, a pardon does not erase the recipient's guilt. In *Burdick v. United States* (1915), the Supreme Court stated in its ruling that someone who accepts a pardon indirectly admits guilt and confesses to the pardoned offense. However, the *Burdick* case involved a petitioner who had refused a pardon from President Woodrow Wilson. The pardon had been granted for the sole purpose of making George Burdick testify in a criminal case, taking away his ability to "plead the Fifth" on the stand. It is still unclear whether a pardoned person necessarily admits guilt by accepting a pardon. A pardoned offense is not removed from someone's criminal record unless it is expunged by a judicial process.

Reprieves

A reprieve is a presidential order to delay a convicted person's punishment. As it is most often used to delay execution for an inmate on death row, it's used primarily by state governors since most death row inmates are guilty of murder, which is a state crime. A reprieve is typically granted to give a convicted person time to gather evidence that might overturn the conviction.

Commutations

A commutation occurs when the president reduces a sentence they believe to be overly harsh or excessive. The pardoning power allows the president to commute (or reduce) a sentence for any federal crime, while keeping the conviction. In 1977, President Jimmy Carter commuted the sentence of G. Gordon Liddy, who had received a twenty-year prison sentence and a $40,000 fine for his role in the Watergate scandal. Carter commuted Liddy's sentence to eight years and left the fine in place. Liddy, who remained a convicted felon after his commutation, occasionally bragged about his wife's extensive gun collection (as a convicted felon, Liddy could not own a firearm).

Amnesties

Occasionally, presidents may extend blanket pardons in the form of general amnesties, giving immunity from further prosecution and punishment to a whole category of offenders. On Christmas Day in 1868, just before leaving office, President Andrew Johnson signed an amnesty proclamation giving a full pardon to all former Confederates. Prior to this, Johnson had pardoned former Confederate leaders on an individual basis. In 1924, President Calvin Coolidge proclaimed amnesty for anyone who had deserted from the military during World War I, as he saw no point in prosecuting or punishing anyone further.

HISTORICAL EXERCISES OF THE PARDONING POWER

The presidential pardon has been used for a number of different reasons. Over the years, presidents have used the pardoning power to reward political supporters, extend an olive branch to political opponents, and close the book on undesirable chapters of American history.

Washington's Pardon of the Whiskey Rebels

President George Washington first used the pardoning power in 1795 after the conclusion of the Whiskey Rebellion. Although Washington had marshaled a large militia force of thirteen thousand men to stop the rebellious forces in Western Pennsylvania with a large show of force, he shifted gears toward reconciliation after the rebellion was dispersed. Two leaders of the Whiskey Rebellion had been found guilty of treason and were sentenced to hang. In pardoning the two men, Washington set a precedent for the generous exercise of clemency in a republic.

Harding's Pardon of Debs

On Christmas Day, President Warren G. Harding commuted the sentence of Eugene V. Debs. Debs had run against Harding in the 1920 election from prison, serving time for urging Americans to resist the draft for World War I. Harding's pardon of Debs shows how the pardoning power can be used to show goodwill to political opponents.

Ford's Pardon of Nixon

Perhaps no presidential pardon has been as controversial or as widely discussed as President Gerald Ford's pardon of Richard Nixon in 1974. Nixon, embroiled in the Watergate scandal, faced potential criminal charges after resigning the presidency to avoid impeachment. Upon his accession to the presidency, Ford, who had served as Nixon's vice president, chose to pardon his disgraced predecessor. Ford's decision to pardon Nixon was a political gamble, intended to close a divisive chapter in American history and end what Ford called America's "long national nightmare." The pardon, however, sparked a national debate on the extent of the pardon power and its moral implications. Ford lost his bid for reelection in 1976 partly due to the American electorate's disapproval of the pardon (though the bad economy likely also played a part).

Clinton's Controversial Pardons

President Bill Clinton raised some eyebrows with several controversial pardons in his last days before leaving office. He ruffled some feathers when he pardoned his brother, Roger Clinton, for drug-related convictions in the 1980s for which he had already served time. Greater controversy surrounded the pardon of billionaire financier Marc Rich, who had been indicted on federal charges of tax evasion and making oil deals with Iran. Although Clinton claimed that legal experts had convinced him that Rich had not committed a crime, there was speculation in the media that the pardon had more to do with Rich's ex-wife's generous donations to the Democratic Party and the Clinton Library. Clinton's pardon of Marc Rich raised serious questions about the role that wealth and political contributions play in pardons.

Pardoning the Turkey

Although the president's power to pardon is typically taken quite seriously, an exception occurs each year around Thanksgiving when the president pardons a Thanksgiving turkey. This charming tradition, typically held in the White House Rose Garden, spares a lucky turkey from becoming a Thanksgiving meal.

A SELF-PARDON?

In recent years, people have wondered whether presidents can pardon themselves. This has become a matter of increasing speculation as President Donald Trump campaigns for another term in office while facing, and being convicted of, federal charges. Could Trump, or another president in a similar position, make charges disappear by pardoning himself? The Constitution's lack of clarity on this matter may call for another look at the pardoning power.

THE TREATY-MAKING POWER

Making Peace and Forging International Agreements

An important function of the executive branch of government is forging peace treaties, alliances, and trade agreements with other nations. However, unlike the pardoning power, which the Constitution grants exclusively to the president, the treaty-making power is a power the president shares with the Senate. It is fitting that this presidential power would have a legislative check, as making an international agreement is a much more momentous endeavor than extending mercy to a single criminal.

THE TREATY CLAUSE

While the Constitution's Treaty Clause grants the president the power to make treaties, it also contains a high bar for Senate approval, ensuring that the Senate is involved in the process of making treaties.

> [The president] shall have Power, by and with the Advice and Consent of the Senate, to make Treaties, provided two thirds of the Senators present concur.
> —Article II, Section 2, Clause 2 of the Constitution

The Constitution requires that treaties receive the Senate's approval by a two-thirds vote. Furthermore, the Constitution states that the Senate is to give both "advice and consent" when it comes to treaties, indicating that the Senate should be consulted by the president during the treaty-making process. In giving the Senate such an extensive role in the treaty-making process, the framers envisioned the Senate performing some of the key functions that had been performed by the Roman Senate for which it was named. When US senators ratify treaties and confirm foreign ambassadors, they perform the same functions that their predecessors in the Roman Senate performed over two thousand years ago.

HISTORIC AMERICAN TREATIES

Over the course of US history, the president and the Senate have collaborated on countless treaties, a handful of which deserve special mention for their historical impact. These treaties have facilitated foreign trade, added land to the United States, and created alliances with other nations.

The Jay Treaty (1795)

The treaty-making power was exercised for the first time in 1794, when the Senate ratified the controversial Jay Treaty with Britain in 1795. The opposition to the Jay Treaty was led by Thomas Jefferson and James Madison. They believed that its terms, which gave Britain "most favored nation" trading status, were too favorable to the British. The Senate ratified the Jay Treaty by a vote of 20–10, exactly the number of votes needed. John Jay remarked later that he believed he could have walked from one end of the country to the other by the light of his burning effigies (representations of political figures that are created in order to be burned in protest).

The Louisiana Purchase Treaty (1803)

During Thomas Jefferson's presidency, American diplomats in France negotiated the Louisiana Purchase Treaty, the first major land acquisition in US history. Before the Louisiana Purchase, the Mississippi River formed the nation's western boundary, and the mouth of the Mississippi River was under foreign control. This left American commerce at the mercy of a foreign power. For only $15 million (which in those days was worth much more than it is today), the United States purchased over eight hundred square miles from France at the unbelievable price of three cents an acre. The land gained from the Louisiana Purchase opened the way for westward expansion, and fifteen new states were eventually created.

An Unconstitutional Treaty?

Although Jefferson wholeheartedly supported the Louisiana Purchase, he was uncertain as to whether the treaty was constitutional, as the Constitution did not authorize the president to purchase land. However, Secretary of State James Madison convinced Jefferson that the Senate's power to ratify treaties was the only check on the president's treaty-making power.

The North Atlantic Treaty (1949)

As the peace established by the end of World War II quickly broke down and the Cold War began to heat up, the United States, Canada, and ten European nations gathered in Washington to sign the North Atlantic Treaty. Article V of the North Atlantic Treaty considers an attack on any member of the North Atlantic Treaty Organization (NATO) to be an attack on every member.

TREATIES WITH INDIAN TRIBES

The Constitution designates Indian tribes as separate nations within the United States by including them in the Commerce Clause and exempting them from taxation by state governments. Between 1778 and 1904, the US government made hundreds of treaties with individual Indian tribes, recognizing the sovereignty of the tribes over their respective jurisdictions, known as reservations. Regrettably, many of these treaties were the result of political and military pressure that the US government placed on tribes, and there have been many instances when the government broke these agreements after they were made. The Indian Removal Act of 1830 authorized President Andrew Jackson to negotiate treaties with the tribes in the southeastern United States that would result in their displacement to present-day Oklahoma. Although this was framed as a legal process, the US government never had any intention of letting the tribes hold on to their ancestral lands.

THE REJECTION OF THE VERSAILLES TREATY

One of the most famous treaties in US history was a treaty that was not ratified. President Woodrow Wilson played a key role in negotiating the Treaty of Versailles, which included his Fourteen Points and the creation of the League of Nations. However, Wilson did not bother to consult the Senate for advice when negotiating the treaty, and he did not bring any senators with him for the negotiations in Paris. When Wilson, a Democrat, presented the treaty to the Republican-controlled Senate for ratification, a national debate ensued over the League of Nations. Many

Americans believed the treaty could undermine American sovereignty by obligating the nation to enter a foreign war without congressional consent. Republican senators offered Wilson a compromise version of the treaty with fourteen reservations, but Wilson refused and instructed Democratic senators to vote against the treaty. Although Wilson received the Nobel Peace Prize for his work in creating the League of Nations, the United States never joined the organization.

THE DECLINE OF TREATIES

In an age of increasing political polarization, in which even foreign policy can take on a political dimension, recent presidents have increasingly bypassed the treaty-making process, opting instead to make executive agreements with their counterparts from other nations. Executive agreements are easier to negotiate than treaties since they do not require the advice and consent of the Senate, but they are also less durable. An example of this is the Paris Agreement, which the United States joined in 2016 via executive agreement at the behest of President Barack Obama. In 2017, President Donald Trump withdrew from the agreement. Although President Joe Biden rejoined in 2021, a future president could easily withdraw from it again.

The president's power to negotiate an executive agreement is limited, as it cannot conflict with the Constitution or federal law and can be nullified by Congress. When the president's party controls both houses of Congress, the president may ask Congress to ratify an executive agreement so that it has the force of the law. That said, the trend toward executive agreements gives the House of Representatives a role in foreign policy that the framers may not have envisioned, showing how the constitutional system of checks and balances can evolve over time.

THE VETO POWER

The President As Legislator

Although most of the president's powers are outlined in Article II of the Constitution, one of the president's most important powers appears in Article I, which gives the president a role in the legislative process through the veto power. The veto (Latin for "I forbid") is a presidential power inherited from the ancient Roman Republic, in which the highest executive officials (the consuls) each could stop legislation from being passed. This power is key to a healthy constitutional republic, as it can keep ill-advised legislation from passing by the vote of bare majorities of each house. The veto power gives the chief executive a powerful check on the legislative branch, which led some to refer to the president as "chief legislator."

THE PRESENTMENT CLAUSE

The description of the legislative process in Article I, Section 7 requires that bills passed by both houses of Congress be presented to the president for consideration before becoming law.

> Every Bill which shall have passed the House of Representatives and the Senate, shall, before it become a Law, be presented to the President of the United States; If he approve[s] he shall sign it, but if not he shall return it, with his Objections to that House in which it shall have originated, who shall enter the Objections at large on their Journal, and proceed to reconsider it.
>
> —Article I, Section 7, Clause 2 of the Constitution

The Presentment Clause requires the president to include a message explaining his objections when vetoing a piece of legislation. The Constitution does not limit the reasons for which a president can veto a bill. Over the years, presidents have vetoed bills due to doubts about constitutionality, concerns about enforcement, and personal distaste.

Rather than waiting for an objectionable piece of legislation to reach their desk, presidents will sometimes use veto threats to influence legislation that is still being drafted and debated in Congress. Veto threats allow presidents to insert themselves into the legislative process at any stage. Such threats often prompt members of Congress to make amendments to the pending legislation to increase the chance of receiving the president's signature.

The "Pocket Veto"

The Constitution gives the president ten days to consider a bill and return it to Congress with either a signature or a veto message. Under normal circumstances, if the president neither signs nor returns the bill to Congress, it becomes law without his signature. However, if Congress adjourns within ten days of passing a bill, a president may "pocket veto" the bill by taking no action.

LIMITATIONS ON THE VETO POWER

Unlike the veto powers of the Roman consuls, the president's veto power is not absolute. The framers not only gave the president a check against the legislative branch in the form of a veto; they also allowed Congress to override a veto by a two-thirds vote of both houses. Such a margin of support reflects a consensus around the legislation that is only possible with broad bipartisan support. The difficulty in reaching this threshold is underscored by the math: Over the entire course of the US government's existence under the Constitution, presidents have vetoed over twenty-five hundred bills, and just over one hundred have been overridden. The presidential veto is not absolute, but, historically, it has been very close.

In addition to giving Congress the ability to override presidential vetoes, the Constitution places further limits on the president's veto power to maintain a balance between the legislative and executive branches.

No Line Item Veto Power

The Constitution gives the president an all-or-nothing choice to either sign a bill "as is" or return it to Congress with a veto message. It does not allow the president to use a line item veto, which would allow the president to veto individual portions (line items) of spending bills while leaving the rest of the legislation intact. Proponents of the line item veto praise it as a check against wasteful spending. Opponents have called it a "Frankenstein veto" because of its potential to make major changes to a bill to produce something different than what legislators intended. Several state constitutions give governors a line item veto, and the short-lived Confederate Constitution gave the power to the Confederate president.

In 1996, Congress passed the Line Item Veto Act. This was signed into law by President Bill Clinton, who used the power to veto individual congressional appropriations (spending items) within bills that he signed into law. In *Clinton v. City of New York* (1998), the Supreme Court declared the Line Item Veto Act to be unconstitutional because it gave the president more power over the legislative process than the framers intended.

Constitutional Amendments

When Congress proposes constitutional amendments, the proposed amendments are sent directly to the states, as the president isn't involved in amending the Constitution. When Congress passed the Thirteenth Amendment in 1865, President Lincoln signed it out of sentiment, believing his signature to be proper even if it was not necessary.

HISTORICAL USE OF THE VETO POWER

The earliest American presidents used the veto power sparingly. In his eight years as president, George Washington only vetoed two bills: a legislative apportionment bill (determining each state's representation in the House) due to doubts about its constitutionality and a military reorganization bill because of objections expressed by his secretary of war. Neither John Adams nor Thomas Jefferson ever used the veto power, as their political parties controlled both houses of Congress during their respective tenures. James Madison vetoed seven pieces of legislation, including John C. Calhoun's "Bonus Bill," which would have distributed funds to the states to finance infrastructure projects. Although Madison personally liked the idea behind the Bonus Bill, he didn't want to set a precedent for passing legislation that had no clear constitutional basis. He recommended that the Constitution be amended first to allow Congress to pay for infrastructure projects.

Andrew Jackson's veto of the bill to recharter the Second Bank of the United States may be the most famous veto in US history. Jackson's lengthy veto message outlined his objections against the Bank of the United States, claiming that the bank's charter infringed on the rights of the states to tax business profits. He saw no role for the government in chartering a for-profit institution that stood to benefit wealthy investors more than the "common man."

The rival Whig Party accused Jackson of abusing the veto power, portraying him in a political cartoon as "King Andrew the First." Although Jackson vetoed twelve bills during his presidency (more than his six predecessors combined), his veto count pales in comparison to those of Grover Cleveland and FDR, both of whom vetoed hundreds of bills while in office. By comparison, recent presidents have used the veto power as much as their predecessors. Since 2001, presidents have averaged less than ten vetoes per four-year term. In the age of televised veto threats, the veto's golden age may have passed.

ELECTING THE PRESIDENT

The Path to the Nation's Most Powerful Office

Presidential politics is a hallmark of the American political system. Every four years, Americans go to the polls to elect a president to serve in the most powerful office in the US government. Although the election happens every four years, presidential campaigns (and their fundraising efforts) dominate the news cycle for nearly half of that period. Furthermore, on election night, Americans follow the election results that are based on a complex formula. This unique and intricate system of presidential politics is rooted in the Constitution.

QUALIFICATIONS FOR OFFICE

The presidency is such an important job that one would think there would be a long list of credentials for it; however, the Constitution only gives three qualifications for the presidency.

> No Person except a natural born Citizen...shall be eligible to the Office of President; neither shall any Person be eligible to that Office who shall not have attained to the Age of thirty five Years, and been fourteen Years a Resident within the United States.
>
> —Article II, Section 1, Clause 5 of the Constitution

These qualifications were designed to ensure that the president would have no foreign loyalties and would have reached sufficient maturity to handle the duties of the office. The three key qualifications are worthy of elaboration.

Natural-Born Citizenship

Although the Constitution does not define natural-born citizenship, it generally refers to a person born on US soil. Some strict definitions of natural-born citizenship require at least one parent to be a citizen, but this interpretation has been rejected. Additionally, Americans born abroad to American parents completing military service are considered natural-born citizens. The constitutional idea of natural-born citizenship was intended to shield the presidency from foreign influence. No one would want someone acting as commander in chief who owed allegiance to a foreign government.

Age Requirement

The president is required to be at least thirty-five years old. At the Constitutional Convention, delegates debated about whether there should be any age requirements for federal office, in general. George Mason of Virginia expressed his belief that a twenty-one-year-old had no business occupying any office in the federal government, believing that a person that inexperienced would express political opinions that would be "too crude and erroneous to merit an influence on public measures." The majority of the delegates agreed and decided to set the ages for the House, the Senate, and the Presidency to twenty-five, thirty, and thirty-five years, respectively. The age limit for the presidency has never been much of an issue, as no one under forty has ever been elected as president or vice president; the median age for presidents when they take office is fifty-five.

Residency Requirement

In addition to being a natural-born citizen, a presidential hopeful must have resided in the United States for at least fourteen years. This requirement was designed to keep someone who was born in the

United States, but had spent most of their life abroad, from assuming the presidency, as such a person may be subject to foreign influence.

ELECTING THE PRESIDENT

The Constitution provides for the election of the president through the Electoral College, the members of which are chosen by each state.

> Each State shall appoint, in such Manner as the Legislature thereof may direct, a Number of Electors, equal to the whole Number of Senators and Representatives to which the State may be entitled in the Congress.
>
> —Article II, Section 1, Clause 2 of the Constitution

To balance the influence of the small and large states, the framers created a formula for the Electoral College that gives the large states more votes and the small states a greater amount of proportional representation in the election of the president. For example, California has fifty-five votes, which is nearly twenty times Wyoming's three votes. However, when divided by the number of residents, California has one electoral vote for every seven hundred thousand residents, while Wyoming gets a vote for every two hundred thousand residents.

In today's democratic republic, many Americans are surprised that the president is not elected through a direct popular election. In fact, five presidents have taken office despite receiving fewer popular votes than their opponents. Abraham Lincoln took office after winning only 40 percent of popular votes cast (he had three opponents). The framers of the Constitution would not have seen these results as problematic, as the Electoral College was designed to create an indirect election for the president that would be shielded from popular opinion. Some people want to replace the Electoral College with a popular vote, but such a change would require a constitutional amendment. Small states, whose voice in presidential elections would be altogether muted if such an amendment passed, would likely oppose it.

CAMPAIGNING FOR PRESIDENT

American presidential campaigns are unlike any other campaigns in the world, lasting longer and costing more money than any other election. Presidential candidates are expected to declare their candidacies more than a year before election day, and candidates spend billions of dollars to get to the White House. This is partly due to the two-party system in the United States. Although political parties are never mentioned in the Constitution, partisan groups materialized quickly in the years following ratification, and Americans have only known one brief period when two organized parties were not competing for the presidency.

While many other nations (like Canada and Mexico) have laws limiting campaigning periods to a number of weeks or months, Congress cannot make such a law. The First Amendment prohibits Congress from limiting freedom of speech, and campaigning for office is a form of protected speech. In *Citizens United v. FEC* (2010), the Supreme Court, in a contested 5–4 decision, ruled that money spent on election advocacy is also a form of speech protected by the First Amendment. Although Congress can limit the amount that an individual or organization contributes to a campaign, it cannot place limits on independent expenditures in favor of candidates. The *Citizens United* decision resulted in the rise of "super PACs," independent political action committees that can spend unlimited money promoting political campaigns (as long as the super PAC and the promoted campaign do not communicate directly).

Although some Americans may wish for a shorter campaign period or a limitation on campaign spending, such changes would require an amendment to the Constitution that would enable Congress to regulate political speech.

THE TWO-TERM LIMIT

The original Constitution did not place any limitation on the number of times the president could be reelected. Upon reading the Constitution for the first time, Thomas Jefferson expressed serious reservations about its lack of a provision for rotation in office. George Washington, sharing Jefferson's belief in the principles of republicanism, chose to step down voluntarily after two terms in office. He was hailed by admirers as an "American Cincinnatus" after the ancient Roman politician who had been given emergency dictatorial power for six months, yet yielded it back after only sixteen days. Every American president followed Washington's two-term precedent until Franklin D. Roosevelt ran for a third (and fourth) term. After FDR's death, the Twenty-Second Amendment was proposed and ratified, adding Washington's unwritten precedent into the written Constitution.

THE STATE OF THE UNION

A Presidential Tradition

A respected high school teacher, a cancer survivor, the spouse of a firefighter who died in the line of duty, and many more have received invitations to Washington, DC, for a once-in-a-lifetime experience: attending the president's annual State of the Union address. But what exactly is the significance of the State of the Union? How are guests selected to attend? And in an age of seemingly unlimited entertainment options, does the State of the Union still matter, or is it a relic from a time when Americans had nothing else to watch on TV?

THE CONSTITUTIONAL MANDATE

Article II, Section 3 of the Constitution requires that the president "from time to time give to the Congress Information of the State of the Union, and recommend to their Consideration such Measures as he shall judge necessary and expedient." In other words, the Constitution requires the president to regularly brief Congress on the country's status and propose necessary and suitable actions. This practice, deeply ingrained in American political tradition, has evolved over time, reflecting changes in communication and technological advancements in mass media.

HISTORICAL EVOLUTION

George Washington set a precedent for delivering the president's annual message to Congress (as it was known then) in person. John

Adams also delivered the annual message in the form of a speech. However, Thomas Jefferson, a soft-spoken man better known for his pen than his oratory, began the practice of sending written messages; he believed that a written message would waste less time than an official presidential appearance before Congress. His decision could have also been rooted in his republican simplicity, desiring to end a practice that may have reminded him of the British monarch's occasional speeches before Parliament. Jefferson's practice of sending written annual messages to Congress continued for over a century.

The Long and the Short of It

George Washington's 1790 annual message to Congress was the first State of the Union address, and it was also the shortest, with just over one thousand words. Jimmy Carter's 1981 annual message, which followed his unsuccessful bid for reelection, was the longest State of the Union address, with over thirty-three thousand words. Carter's final annual message is also the last message to be submitted to Congress in writing.

In 1913, Woodrow Wilson, a professor-turned-politician who was accustomed to giving speeches, decided to deliver his annual message to Congress in person. Other presidents followed suit on radio and television, taking advantage of the opportunity to deliver the annual message both to Congress and the American people. The term "State of the Union Address" was first coined by Franklin D. Roosevelt and officially adopted by Harry Truman, whose 1947 address was the first to be televised. In 1965, Lyndon Johnson became the first president to deliver the address on prime time, increasing its impact to the point that the opposing party began the tradition of delivering a televised response to the State of the Union the following year. The opposing party's response to the State of the Union has become a key part of the event, highlighting a democratic commitment to open conversation.

MEMORABLE MOMENTS

Over the years, presidents have used their State of the Union addresses to break news, claim credit for their accomplishments, and lay out major policy proposals before Congress. In 1848, James K. Polk's Fourth Annual Message sparked the California Gold Rush when he informed Congress that the gold deposits were "more extensive and valuable than was anticipated." Nearly one hundred thousand people journeyed to California the following year. Lincoln's second annual message was praised for its powerful prose that encouraged the nation in the midst of the Civil War and rallied support for his Emancipation Proclamation. Franklin D. Roosevelt used his 1941 State of the Union address to challenge prevailing isolationist sentiments in the United States, envisioning a role for the country in protecting the "Four Freedoms" (of speech, of worship, from want, and from fear) across the globe.

The Designated Survivor

An interesting aspect of the modern-day State of the Union is that one cabinet member always skips the event. This practice, known as the "designated survivor" policy, ensures that if a catastrophic event incapacitates the president and other key officials present, there is someone ready to assume leadership.

Some traditions relating to the State of the Union address are relatively recent, with several elements originating with Ronald Reagan, a former actor known as the "Great Communicator." In his 1982 State of the Union address, he recognized Lenny Skutnik, whom he had invited to attend as his personal guest. After a plane crashed into the Potomac River on an icy January morning, Skutnik plunged into the freezing river to save a passenger who would have drowned without his intervention. The heartwarming story went over so well that the tradition of presidents recognizing "Skutniks"—everyday American heroes—during the State of the Union continues to this day. The following year, Reagan coined the phrase "The State of the Union is strong," which has been widely repeated by presidents since.

STILL RELEVANT TODAY?

In recent years, the relevance and impact of the State of the Union address have been increasingly questioned. While sixty-six million Americans tuned in for Bill Clinton's first State of the Union address in 1993, today's addresses have drawn barely half of that live audience. In the digital age, Americans (especially younger generations) increasingly eschew live broadcasts, preferring to digest summaries and brief sound bites after the fact. The State of the Union remains a vital platform for presidents to articulate their vision and legislative agenda; however, Congress can just as easily ignore the president's requests (especially when controlled by the opposing party). Although the State of the Union address may not be as popular now, it's unlikely that presidents will return to sending written remarks to Congress anytime soon.

IMPEACHING THE PRESIDENT

High Crimes and Misdemeanors

As recently as 1997, no living American had ever witnessed a presidential impeachment. However, Americans have witnessed three impeachments in the last quarter century. The idea of impeachment is still nebulous to many Americans, many of whom believe that impeachment is synonymous with removal from office or that it has the force of a criminal proceeding. At the time of publication, no American president has ever been removed from office by the impeachment process. Nevertheless, impeachment makes a great story for today's media and the history books, so it's advantageous to understand the process.

WHAT IS IMPEACHMENT?

In constitutional terms, impeachment is a formal charge of misconduct against a federal official by a majority vote of the House of Representatives. It results in a trial by the US Senate. Informally, impeachment can describe any attempt to undermine someone's integrity, as an attorney who is cross-examining a witness might try to "impeach" a witness in court by catching them in a lie. The word comes from a medieval Latin word, *impedicare*, which means to catch or entangle. So, while impeachment is not the same thing as removal from office, it can catch a federal official and lead to their removal.

The Constitution outlines the grounds for impeachment in Article II, Section 4, which states: "The President, Vice President, and all civil Officers of the United States, shall be removed from Office on Impeachment for, and Conviction of, Treason, Bribery, or other high Crimes and Misdemeanors." While this clause clearly defines treason and bribery as grounds for impeachment, there is ongoing debate as to what constitutes "high Crimes and Misdemeanors." In criminal law, a misdemeanor is a minor crime, such as disorderly conduct or reckless driving, so this leaves room for interpretation regarding what constitutes an impeachable offense.

THE IMPEACHMENT PROCESS

The Constitution divides impeachment powers between the two houses of Congress. Article I, Section 2 grants the "sole Power of Impeachment" to the House of Representatives, meaning that only the House can initiate the impeachment process by a simple majority vote. Once the House passes articles of impeachment, Article I, Section 3 grants the Senate "the sole Power to try all Impeachments." If the president is impeached, the chief justice presides over the trial instead of the vice president. The Constitution sets a high bar for removal from office, stating that "no Person shall be convicted without the Concurrence of two thirds of the Members present."

A guilty verdict in the Senate results in the federal official's removal from office, and the Senate has the discretion to bar a convicted individual from ever holding office again. The Constitution only grants the Senate jurisdiction over office holding. An individual removed from office through the impeachment process does not become a criminal, but they can be subject to prosecution for criminal charges through standard judicial proceedings for the same offenses.

NOT JUST THE PRESIDENT

Although presidential impeachments gain the most attention, any federal official can be impeached. Of the twenty-one federal officials who have been impeached, fifteen have been federal judges. Additionally, all eight federal officials who have been successfully removed from office through impeachment have been federal judges. Only one member of Congress has ever been impeached; both houses have internal provisions for expelling their own members.

PRESIDENTIAL IMPEACHMENTS

Since the ratification of the Constitution, only three presidents have been impeached: Andrew Johnson, Bill Clinton, and Donald Trump. Although no impeachment proceeding against a president has ever been successful to date, the impeachment of a president is always a matter of great intrigue and importance.

In the 1864 election, Abraham Lincoln opted for bipartisan appeal, hoping to unify the electorate during a wartime election by choosing Andrew Johnson, a Southern Democrat who had opposed secession, as his running mate. After Lincoln's assassination, Andrew Johnson became a Democratic president facing a Republican-controlled Congress.

Congressional Republicans, afraid that Johnson would attempt to replace Lincoln's cabinet with Democratic appointees, passed the Tenure of Office Act, which required the president to have the Senate's approval in order to dismiss a cabinet official. When Johnson dismissed Secretary of War Edwin Stanton, the House impeached Johnson for violating the Tenure of Office Act. The

Republican-controlled Senate acquitted Johnson by a vote of 35–19 (one vote short of the two-thirds threshold to convict). Johnson was saved by the votes of ten moderate Republicans who joined every Democratic senator in voting "not guilty."

Johnson's impeachment established a number of precedents for presidential impeachment trials. First, there was a great deal of public interest. Additionally, impeachment was demonstrated to be a politically driven process, with most Republicans in favor and nearly all Democrats opposed. Finally, if Johnson had been convicted, it would have set a precedent for Congress, when controlled by one party, to remove presidents of the opposing party for political reasons. Fortunately, this didn't happen.

Nixon: A Common Misconception

Some Americans are prone to identify Richard Nixon as a president who has been impeached. Contrary to popular belief, Nixon was never formally impeached. Facing almost certain impeachment and conviction due to the Watergate scandal, Nixon chose to resign from office to avoid facing impeachment, becoming the only US president to do so.

It was over a century before a president was impeached again, when the House of Representatives impeached Bill Clinton for perjury (lying under oath) and obstruction of justice in connection with his extramarital relationship with Monica Lewinsky, a White House intern. As with Andrew Johnson, the articles of impeachment were passed by a Republican-controlled House, with only a handful of Democrats voting in favor of impeachment and a small number of Republicans voting in opposition. Clinton's impeachment took place during the era of continuous cable television coverage, and Americans followed the drama from home. In a pattern similar to the Johnson impeachment, the Senate acquitted Clinton on both charges, with a handful of moderate Republicans joining every Democrat in voting not guilty. Neither charge was supported by a majority of the Senate. The impeachment of Bill Clinton marked the first time that a president was impeached for misconduct stemming from a personal scandal, showing that a president is vulnerable to impeachment on a number of fronts.

As of 2024, Donald Trump is the only president to have been impeached twice. His first impeachment occurred in 2019, when the House of Representatives passed articles of impeachment for obstruction of Congress and abuse of power related to a phone call between Trump and Ukrainian president Volodymyr Zelenskyy, in which Trump allegedly encouraged the foreign leader to prosecute the son of his political rival, Joe Biden. Following previous patterns, the House passed the articles of impeachment along partisan lines, with every Republican joining a handful of Democrats in voting against it. However, something unprecedented happened in the Senate: One Republican senator joined the Democrats in voting in favor of removal from office. This marked the first time that a senator from the president's party voted to convict in a presidential impeachment. During Trump's second impeachment, which was due to inciting insurrection in connection with the January 6 riot at the US Capitol, seven Republican senators joined every Democrat in voting to convict, but the fifty-seven votes in favor of removal were still ten shy of the sixty-seven necessary.

The second Trump impeachment raised a constitutional question regarding whether a president could be impeached after he left office. Most Republican senators argued that the Senate did not have the constitutional jurisdiction to try Trump after his term ended. However, the majority of the Senate voted in favor of the trial's constitutionality, setting a precedent for trying a president who has already left office.

THE VICE PRESIDENCY

Waiting in the Wings

Of all of the officials in the executive branch of government, the Constitution only mentions two: the president and the vice president. The vice president occupies the second-most important office in the executive branch and assumes the presidency in the event of the death, resignation, removal, or temporary incapacity of the president. This role pales in comparison to the presidency, prompting many to refuse the office. In having no set executive branch responsibilities, the vice presidency threatens to cast politicians into obscurity; however, it also may elevate people to the presidency that otherwise might never have attained it.

PRESIDENT OF THE SENATE

The Vice President of the United States shall be President of the Senate, but shall have no Vote, unless they be equally divided.
—Article I, Section 3, Clause 4 of the Constitution

When the president is alive and in good health, the vice president only has one constitutional responsibility: presiding over the Senate. By assigning this duty to the vice president, the Constitution gives the vice president a role in the Senate that comes without Senate membership. Also, the Constitution gives the president full discretion concerning the vice president's role within the executive branch. Although George Washington respected his vice president, John Adams, he excluded him from the cabinet because of his duties in the legislative branch. As a result, Adams found himself isolated and without a real place in the government. In a letter to his wife, Abigail, he wrote: "My country has in its wisdom contrived for me the most insignificant office that ever the invention of man contrived or his imagination conceived."

SUCCESSOR TO THE PRESIDENT

> In Case of the Removal of the President from Office, or of his Death, Resignation, or Inability to discharge the Powers and Duties of the said Office, the Same shall devolve on the Vice President.
>
> —Article II, Section 1, Clause 6 of the Constitution

John Adams might have languished in the obscurity of the vice presidency; however, his patience paid off, as he became the first American politician to use the vice presidency to step into the presidency. In 1796, Adams was elected as the second US president. When Thomas Jefferson, who had served as Adams's vice president, defeated him in 1800, he became the second person to advance directly from the vice presidency to the presidency. However, this trend was short-lived, as it was not until Martin Van Buren succeeded Andrew Jackson in 1836 that another vice president would be elected president. In the postwar era, three former vice presidents (Richard Nixon, George H. W. Bush, and Joe Biden) were elected after serving under presidents who had completed full terms. So advancing from vice president to president is not a surefire chain of events, by any means.

Of the fifteen vice presidents who assumed the presidency, nine took the most obvious path: the death or resignation of a president.

In 1841, John Tyler assumed the presidency after President William Henry Harrison died of pneumonia only one month after taking office. However, Tyler was then dubbed "His Accidency" because of his unelected ascendancy to the presidency. He was the first president to have a veto overridden by Congress and the only president to be kicked out of his own party. Sadly, neither party nominated him for president in 1844. During the nineteenth century, four vice presidents succeeded presidents who died in office. None of them were ever elected themselves.

In the twentieth century, vice presidents took center stage after patiently "waiting in the wings" during the presidencies of their predecessors. President Theodore Roosevelt took office after the assassination of William McKinley in 1901. Not only was Roosevelt elected to a full term in his own right in 1904; he is also remembered for passing essential legislation like the Meat Inspection Act and the Pure Food and Drug Act. Both Calvin Coolidge and Harry Truman were elected after succeeding presidents who died in office. Lyndon Johnson, who assumed the presidency after the Kennedy assassination, steered ambitious civil rights legislation like the Civil Rights Act of 1964 and the Voting Rights Act of 1968. Elected in 1964, Johnson lost popularity during the Vietnam War and did not seek reelection in 1968.

THE TWELFTH AMENDMENT

Originally, the Constitution called for each member of the Electoral College to cast two votes on a single ballot, with both votes being tallied to determine the president and the vice president. The original formula seemed simple: The person with the most electoral votes would become president and the second-place finisher would be vice president. The framers of the Constitution did not envision that presidential elections would become the partisan political contests of today. The principles of classical republicanism discourage political parties because they place the interests of factions over the whole.

Despite the framers' optimism, two political parties had materialized by the time Washington (who had twice been elected unanimously) stepped down from the presidency. In 1796, John Adams, the Federalist Party candidate, defeated Thomas Jefferson of the Democratic-Republican Party, in the first contested presidential election. However, Jefferson finished a close second, resulting in his election as vice president. The election of political rivals as president and vice president created an unanticipated, awkward political arrangement.

The presidential election of 1800 resulted in a far more uncomfortable situation than the one before it. While Jefferson managed to defeat John Adams in a close rematch, Jefferson's electors exercised extreme party discipline, with every Democratic-Republican elector casting their votes for Jefferson and his running mate, Aaron Burr. These electors had presumed that Burr would concede the election to Jefferson and be vice president. When Burr refused, it sent the vote to the House of Representatives, where Jefferson was elected after much fanfare.

The elections of 1796 and 1800 demonstrated a need to change the way that the president and vice president were elected. The Twelfth Amendment, which directs electors to vote for the president and vice president on separate ballots, was ratified in 1804.

ASSISTANT AND ADVISOR TO THE PRESIDENT

Although the vice president has no set role within the executive branch, twentieth-century presidents began involving their vice presidents more in their administrations. In 1921, Warren G. Harding became the first president to invite his vice president, Calvin Coolidge, to attend cabinet meetings. (This is now a standard practice.) Dwight D. Eisenhower, who won the presidency despite never holding a political office, relied heavily on his vice president, Richard Nixon, who had served in both houses of Congress. George W. Bush and Barack Obama, both of whom assumed office with no foreign policy experience, chose their vice presidents (Dick Cheney and Joe Biden, respectively) due to their extensive experience in the federal government. Both Biden and Cheney served as key advisors to their younger counterparts. Recently, the vice president has helped to bridge the gap between the president and factions within their party that were skeptical of their nominations. Donald Trump chose Mike Pence to gain credibility with evangelical voters, and Joe Biden chose Kamala Harris, a progressive Democrat who balanced Biden's reputation as a political moderate.

Madame Vice President

In 2021, Vice President Kamala Harris broke two notable barriers for women in American politics. When she was sworn in on January 20, she became the first woman to serve as vice president of the United States. Later in the same year, she became the first woman to exercise presidential power while President Biden was under anesthesia for a medical procedure that lasted about ninety minutes.

Chapter 5

The Judicial Branch

One of the most memorable stories about King Solomon, the biblical ruler of ancient Israel, placed him at the center of a difficult dispute between two women over a baby they each claimed as their own. As no judge had been able to settle the case, the dispute had been brought before the king. Solomon, known for his wisdom, famously asked for a sword so that he could cut the baby in half, giving one half to each woman. One of the women begged that the baby be kept alive and given to the other woman. The king then judged in her favor, knowing her to be the real mother.

King Solomon's judgment hearkens back to an era when kings not only made and executed the laws but also presided over the court of highest appeal. In a democratic republic, this kind of concentration of power is rejected, placing judicial power in the hands of judges who act independently of the legislative and executive branches. The independent judicial branch functions as the third of the three branches of government established by the Constitution.

THE JUDICIAL POWER

Creating an Independent Judiciary

In keeping with Montesquieu's prescription of separation of powers, the framers of the Constitution created a judicial branch designed to be independent of the legislative and executive branches of government. The Constitution created a novel federal court system that did not exist under the Articles of Confederation.

THE JUDICIAL POWER

The judicial Power of the United States, shall be vested in one supreme Court, and in such inferior Courts as the Congress may from time to time ordain and establish.

—Article III, Section 1, Clause 1 of the Constitution

The Constitution does not clearly describe what exactly is meant by the judicial power given to the Supreme Court, making the Court's specific powers ambiguous. This lack of description has given the Supreme Court some flexibility to determine its own authority. Congress also has a great deal of flexibility in organizing the federal court system, as the Supreme Court is the only federal court that must exist according to the Constitution.

SUPREME AND INFERIOR COURTS

The Constitution vests judicial power in the Supreme Court and inferior courts that Congress "may from time to time ordain and establish." Congress has used this power to create federal district and circuit courts.

District Courts

The federal court system is currently organized into ninety-four federal districts. Federal district courts have original jurisdiction over nearly all cases that are filed in the federal court system. Each state has at least one federal district, while some of the larger states, such as New York, Texas, and California, are divided into four federal court districts.

Circuit Courts of Appeal

Congress has also created eleven federal judicial circuits, with each circuit having a court of appeal. For example, someone appealing a verdict reached in a federal district in northern Texas would file the appeal with the Fifth Circuit Court of Appeals, which deals with appeals from Texas, Louisiana, and Mississippi. The largest federal circuit in terms of both geography and caseload is the Ninth Circuit, which includes California and eight other states in the western portion of the United States (including Alaska and Hawaii). In addition to the eleven circuits that encompass the states and federal overseas territories, Washington, DC, has its own federal circuit. Additionally, a separate Federal Circuit Court of Appeals hears all appeals on cases regarding patents, trademarks, and veterans' benefits regardless of where such cases originated geographically.

AN INDEPENDENT JUDICIARY

The judicial branch is unique in that none of its members are elected. Article II, Section 2 of the Constitution gives the president the power to nominate federal judges with the advice and consent of the Senate. Additionally, federal judges do not have terms in office, serving "on good behavior," which means that a federal judge's tenure ends only with their death, retirement, or removal through impeachment. The framers designed the judiciary to be independent of the political branches. Antifederalists were skeptical of a judicial branch that had no direct reliance on the people. However, in Federalist No. 78, Alexander Hamilton argued that the independence of the judiciary was a necessary safeguard against any attempt Congress might make to exceed its constitutional authority.

Hamilton also referred to the judicial branch as the "least dangerous to the political rights of the Constitution; because it will be least in a capacity to annoy or injure them." Hamilton's assessment shows that the framers did not anticipate the judicial branch's current degree of power.

JURISDICTION OF FEDERAL COURTS

Given the federal nature of the US government established by the Constitution, federal courts only have jurisdiction in cases that are not generally the province of state courts. Court cases that fall under federal jurisdiction include cases in which the US government is a party, legal disputes between two or more states (such as disputes over shared waterways), and cases that involve violations of federal laws.

ORIGINAL AND APPELLATE JURISDICTION

The Constitution defines the Supreme Court's original and appellate jurisdiction:

> In all Cases affecting Ambassadors, other public Ministers and Consuls, and those in which a State shall be Party, the supreme Court shall have original Jurisdiction. In all the other Cases before mentioned, the supreme Court shall have appellate Jurisdiction.
>
> —Article III, Section 2, Clause 2 of the Constitution

A court has original jurisdiction when it has the right to hear the initial trial, and a court with appellate jurisdiction has the right to hear appeals against judgments of lower courts with original jurisdiction. Since the Constitution only gives the Supreme Court original jurisdiction over a select few types of cases, nearly all of the cases that are brought before the Supreme Court are brought before it on appeal. When the Supreme Court is presented with a case in which it has original jurisdiction, such as when one state sues another state, the Court has no option but to hear the case. In cases of appellate jurisdiction, the Supreme Court can be very selective, hearing only those cases to which it grants a writ of certiorari (a petition for judicial review). Every year, the Court receives around seven thousand petitions for writs of certiorari. Of those thousands of cases, less than one hundred will be granted certiorari.

THE COMPENSATION CLAUSE

> The Judges, both of the supreme and inferior Courts...shall, at stated Times, receive for their Services, a Compensation, which shall not be diminished during their Continuance in Office.
>
> —Article III, Section 1 of the Constitution

The Compensation Clause of Article III preserves the independence of the judiciary by placing a check on the appropriations powers of Congress. While Congress may increase the compensation of federal judges, it may not decrease a federal judge's compensation during their time in office. Without the Compensation Clause, Congress could pressure a federal judge to resign by reducing their compensation (or even eliminating it altogether).

JUDICIAL REVIEW

It may come as a surprise that the Constitution never explicitly grants federal judges the power to strike down federal laws. The Supreme Court first asserted the power of judicial review in *Marbury v. Madison* (1803) over a decade after the Constitution was ratified. "It is emphatically the province and duty of the judicial department to say what the law is," Chief Justice John Marshall wrote in the unanimous opinion of the Court. In Marshall's view, the Constitution's vestment of judicial power in the Supreme Court included the power to declare a law void if the Court found it to be "repugnant to the Constitution."

The Supreme Court's power of judicial review has elevated it from the "least dangerous" branch of government to a coequal branch of government with a powerful check to wield against the legislative and executive branches. Judicial review has become part of America's constitutional framework because it has been largely accepted by the American people. Congress has never passed laws attempting to limit it (although some measures, such as requiring a two-thirds majority to strike down laws, have been discussed). Occasionally, there is public outcry against individual Supreme Court decisions, but the Supreme Court's power to review laws and executive actions has yet to be seriously challenged.

THE SUPREME COURT

A Look at the Nation's Highest Court

The Supreme Court is the only federal court whose existence is prescribed by the Constitution. However, the Constitution never specifies how many justices will be on the Supreme Court (and doesn't call them justices). The nine-justice Supreme Court that is so familiar to Americans today did not always exist in the way it does now. Also, while the offices of the president, vice president, and speaker of the House of Representatives are all included in the Constitution, there is no mention of the office of chief justice. It's been a long journey on the road to the Supreme Court's current prominence.

JUSTICES OF THE SUPREME COURT

In 1789, the First US Congress had the monumental task of organizing the federal judiciary in accordance with the vague guidelines prescribed by the Constitution. The Judiciary Act of 1789 was the first act that gave structure to the federal judiciary and the Supreme Court. It was this act that specified that the judges who sit on the Supreme Court would be called justices and that they would be led by a chief justice.

The Chief Justice

The chief justice is the official leader of the Supreme Court. No matter when the chief justice joins the Supreme Court, this individual is the senior official from day one, sitting in the center chair and presiding over the body. In accordance with congressional legislation, the president nominates someone specifically for the position of chief justice. This serves as a check on the Supreme Court, as its leader is chosen by a consensus of the president and the Senate rather than by the Court's own members. While some presidents have opted to elevate an associate justice to the position of chief justice, most of the seventeen men who have served as chief justice took their offices as newcomers to the Supreme Court. Although the chief justice is seen as the leader of the Supreme Court, this leadership role is that of the first among equals, as the chief justice casts only one vote out of nine in deciding cases that come before the Court.

Associate Justices

The chief justice is joined by eight associate justices. In photos of the Supreme Court, the associate justices are arranged by order of seniority. The four justices with the most seniority sit on either side of the chief justice, and the four justices with the shortest tenure stand in the back. The senior associate justice, who has the longest tenure on the Court, always sits to the chief justice's right and presides over the Court in the absence of the chief justice.

The Importance of Seniority

Although each justice has an equal vote, seniority plays a major role in the Supreme Court's proceedings. When the justices meet to express their opinions on cases that have been argued before the Court, each justice declares their vote in order of seniority. The chief justice always has seniority regardless of tenure. Seniority is important when assigning authorship of the opinion of the Court. When the chief justice is in the majority, they assign the opinion to a justice of their choice. When the chief justice is not in the majority, the opinion is assigned by the most senior justice who is part of the majority.

THE NUMBER OF JUSTICES

Although the Supreme Court has had nine justices since 1869, this is the result of congressional legislation, as nothing in the Constitution specifies the size of the Supreme Court. The Judiciary Act of 1789 specified that there would be six justices on the Supreme Court, with one of these justices being the chief justice and the other five being associate justices. During the first century of the federal government's existence under the Constitution, the number of justices has been changed multiple times through congressional legislation.

Judiciary Act of 1801

Known by its opponents as the "Midnight Judges Act," the Judiciary Act of 1801 enabled President John Adams, who had lost the 1800 presidential election, to nominate several new federal judges whose political views aligned with the outgoing Federalist Party. One of the new judges was to be a Supreme Court justice, with the number of justices being raised to seven. Over the next decade, Congress would then reduce the number back to six before raising it again to seven.

Judiciary Act of 1837

The first time the Supreme Court had nine justices was in 1837 when Congress created two new judicial circuits to accommodate the westward expansion of the United States. At the time, each Supreme Court justice was in charge of a federal circuit, which they were required to visit at regular intervals in a practice known as circuit riding.

Tenth Circuit Act of 1863

During Abraham Lincoln's presidency, Congress created a tenth judicial circuit and increased the Supreme Court's size to ten in order to accommodate the new circuit. The ten-justice Court established by the 1863 law is the largest the Supreme Court has ever been.

Judicial Circuits Act of 1866

In 1866, the Republican-controlled Congress passed the Judicial Circuits Act, which reduced the number of judicial circuits to nine and lowered the number of justices to seven. This was a political move to stop Andrew Johnson (a Democrat) from nominating any Supreme Court justices. It also eliminated the previous link between the number of circuits and justices.

Circuit Judges Act of 1869

After President Ulysses S. Grant's election, the Republican-controlled Congress passed the Circuit Judges Act of 1869, which increased the number of justices to nine. This marked the last time Congress changed the number of justices on the Supreme Court.

A COURT WITHOUT A HOME

Today, Americans associate the US Capitol Building exclusively with Congress. When the building was completed in 1800, however, the Supreme Court was given space in the basement. In 1859, the current Senate Chamber was completed, allowing the Supreme Court to move to the Old Senate Chamber. Although the Old Senate Chamber was a step up from the basement, it was still a hand-me-down from the legislative branch.

In 1921, William Howard Taft assumed the office of chief justice, becoming the only former president of the United States to also serve on the Supreme Court. Taft used his political connections to convince Congress to give the Supreme Court a permanent home. In 1935, the Supreme Court moved to its current home, a grand neoclassical structure that showcases the judicial branch's dignity as being on par with the legislative and executive branches.

THE SUPREME COURT IN HISTORY

The Supreme Court has gone through a number of phases over the years, and its historical eras are typically designated by the names of the chief justices who presided over the Court during each era. Some of the more influential eras of the Supreme Court include the following:

- **The Marshall Court:** In the early 1800s, Chief Justice John Marshall helped transform the Supreme Court into a formidable governing institution. Marshall's philosophy emphasized a loose construction of the Constitution that expanded federal powers over commerce and the financial sector.
- **The Hughes Court:** Chief Justice Charles Evans Hughes presided over the Court during the New Deal era, in which Congress passed legislation that expanded the role of the federal government. In the early years of the New Deal, the Court was dominated by the "Four Horsemen," a conservative voting bloc that struck down many New Deal policies. Although FDR's "court-packing plan" failed, he was eventually able to change the composition of the Court over time without changing the number of justices. By

the time Hughes retired in 1941, the majority of Supreme Court justices supported New Deal legislation.

- **The Warren Court:** California governor Earl Warren's tenure as chief justice marked the Court's most liberal era. Between 1953 and 1969, the Warren Court decided key cases regarding school segregation, civil rights, and the rights of the accused.
- **The Rehnquist Court:** William Rehnquist, a conservative elevated to chief justice during Ronald Reagan's tenure, presided over an era during which the Supreme Court began a rightward shift away from its midcentury liberal era. The Rehnquist Court popularized the judicial philosophy of New Federalism, often siding with the states against the federal government.
- **The Roberts Court:** Since 2005, Chief Justice John Roberts has presided over a Supreme Court that has increasingly been dominated by Republican-appointed justices. The Roberts Court has made landmark decisions regarding campaign finance, gun rights, and reproductive rights.

Thurgood Marshall

When Thurgood Marshall delivered his oral arguments to the Supreme Court in the *Brown v. Board of Education* case in 1952, he would have had no idea that in another fifteen years, one of those nine seats in front of him would be his. In 1967, President Lyndon Johnson nominated Marshall to be the first African American justice of the Supreme Court.

DURING GOOD BEHAVIOR

The Life Tenure of Federal Judges

The original Constitution did not limit any elected official's tenure of office, although the Constitution requires members of the elected branches to stand for reelection every two, four, or six years. In contrast, federal judges holding their offices under the Constitution serve "on good behavior," a phrase that is understood to mean that they hold their offices until death, retirement, or removal from office by the impeachment process for misconduct in office.

THE GOOD BEHAVIOR CLAUSE

The life tenure of federal judges is established by the Good Behavior Clause (Article III, Section 1) of the Constitution, which reads: "The Judges, both of the supreme and inferior Courts, shall hold their Offices during good Behaviour."

Most states limit the tenure of judges through various methods (e.g., election and mandatory retirement ages), but the Constitution guarantees all federal judges, including Supreme Court justices, what is effectively a life tenure. On one hand, this life tenure might indicate that federal judges are completely unaccountable to the people, as they're also not elected. On the other hand, the framers saw life tenure as a necessary check on the elected branches that would function the same as the Compensation Clause, prohibiting Congress from reducing judicial salaries. Congress would then be limited in its mechanisms for intimidating federal judges.

Behind the Times

The Good Behavior Clause has resulted in the Supreme Court being out of step with the elected branches of government. While the composition of the House of Representatives reflects the political leanings of the electorate at the time of the most recent biennial election, the Supreme Court justices provide nine snapshots of the political leanings of the president and the Senate taken over a period of thirty to forty years. This often leads to the Supreme Court being out of step with the times, frustrating presidents whose legislative agendas encounter opposition from justices appointed by presidents with differing political philosophies. However, this was exactly what the framers intended when they designed the judiciary to be a check against temporary swings in public opinion.

In Federalist No. 78, Alexander Hamilton wrote that the life tenure of federal judges would ensure the "steady, upright, and impartial administration of the laws." While this may be true of judges who exercise their duties without partisanship, this provision of the Constitution can also protect and insulate federal judges who are known to make partisan rulings.

JUDICIAL IMPEACHMENTS

It was initially thought that the impeachment process might be a remedy against the exercise of extreme partisanship by federal judges. When Thomas Jefferson assumed the presidency in 1801 as part of the so-called Revolution of 1800—the first time the reins of government passed from one political party to another—Jefferson sought to use the impeachment process to clean house. The Jeffersonians started with the successful impeachment of Judge John

Pickering, a federal district judge appointed by George Washington, who was removed from office for being drunk on the bench and making unlawful rulings. Jefferson's next target was a big fish: Supreme Court Justice Samuel Chase. Chase was impeached by the House on the basis of eight different incidents that indicated extreme partisanship on the bench. The Senate, although dominated by Jefferson's party, acquitted Chase on all counts, establishing that neither partisanship nor partiality constituted grounds for impeachment.

Jefferson's failed attempt to purge the Supreme Court of its most biased partisan justice demonstrated the limits of the Good Behavior Clause, essentially guaranteeing that federal judges will continue their tenure unless they commit a felony offense such as treason or soliciting bribes. In total, eight federal judges have been removed from office by the impeachment process under the Constitution. All of these judges were found guilty of misconduct that extended beyond incompetence or partisanship. Additionally, neither insanity nor dementia constitute valid grounds for removing a federal judge, as these states of mind do not in and of themselves constitute immoral or criminal acts.

Life Expectancies

When the Constitution was written, the average life expectancy was around thirty-five years of age. Today, Americans live to seventy-seven on average. Although George Washington's death at the age of sixty-seven may seem a bit premature by today's standards, he lived quite a long life by the standards of his time. In short, the framers never could have imagined that it would become the norm for Supreme Court justices to continue to serve on the federal bench into their eighties.

JUDICIAL RETIREMENTS

Other countries, such as Canada, Great Britain, and Germany, have mandatory retirement ages for judges that range between sixty-five and seventy-five. In many cases, these requirements were enacted in the twentieth century as life expectancies convinced legislators that it was not beneficial for judges to serve into their eighties. However, the Constitution's Good Behavior Clause prohibits the United States from enacting a judicial retirement age at the federal level. Most states, whose judicial systems are not bound by this constitutional clause that applies only to federal judges, have set judicial retirement ages between seventy and seventy-five.

The Good Behavior Clause has led to a rise in strategic retirements on the Supreme Court. This trend was seen most recently in the retirements of Justices Anthony Kennedy and Stephen Breyer, both of whom retired from the Court in their eighties. Justice Kennedy, a Reagan appointee, retired in 2018, when Republicans held both the presidency and the Senate, and Justice Breyer, a Clinton appointee, retired in 2022, when Democrats held both the presidency and the Senate. There have been times, however, when Mother Nature intervened before a justice could retire strategically, such as when Justice Ruth Bader Ginsburg, a Clinton appointee, died at the age of eighty-seven in the last months of the Trump administration. President Trump's nomination of Amy Coney Barrett tilted the balance of the Supreme Court by replacing one of the Court's most liberal justices with a conservative.

A FOUNTAIN OF YOUTH

The Good Behavior Clause has also prompted presidents to nominate younger justices to the Supreme Court than was customary in generations past. Chief Justices Earl Warren, Warren Burger, and William Rehnquist were all nominated for their positions in their sixties; however, Chief Justice John Roberts was only fifty when President George W. Bush nominated him for the office. Bush's father, George H. W. Bush, nominated forty-three-year-old Clarence Thomas as an associate justice, ensuring the presence of a reliably conservative voice on the Court for over thirty years. The practice of nominating younger individuals to the Supreme Court allows presidents to construct long-lasting legacies. However, these attempts at legacy building can be unpredictable, as when President George H.W. Bush's other nominee to the Supreme Court, David Souter, drifted to the left early in his tenure, supplying the Court's liberal wing with a reliable vote for nineteen years. Souter retired from the Supreme Court in 2009 at the beginning of Barack Obama's presidency, ensuring that his successor would be nominated by a Democratic president and confirmed by a Democratic Senate.

TREASON AGAINST THE UNITED STATES

Following the Footsteps of Benedict Arnold

In addition to its vague directives regarding the organization of the federal judiciary, Article III of the Constitution also defines treason against the United States and sets guidelines for the punishment of traitors. Treason is the most serious federal offense and is one of two crimes (the other being murder) that is generally considered to be a capital offense. The Constitution's definition of treason has its roots in the American Revolution as well as Americans' experience of tyranny under British rule.

ARNOLD: THE ARCHETYPE OF A TRAITOR

Any mention of treason against the United States hearkens back to General Benedict Arnold, who distinguished himself as a hero and patriot during the Revolutionary War…until he didn't. While bravely leading Continental soldiers into the Battle of Saratoga, Arnold's horse was shot out from under him. His leg was crushed, making him unfit for battlefield service. Expecting to receive gratitude from his country, he was severely disappointed when the Continental Congress showered credit for the victory at Saratoga on Arnold's superior officer. Congress then conducted a politically motivated investigation into Arnold's finances, concluding that he owed a large sum of money to Congress. Arnold, as revenge, secretly conspired with British officers to hand over the fortress at West Point where Arnold had been placed in command. In doing so, Benedict Arnold made war against the United States by giving aid and comfort to the enemy. George Washington, who had once had great faith in Arnold as an officer, made sure the traitor's reputation never recovered.

TREASON UNDER THE ARTICLES

The designation of an offense of treason against the United States was a new development under the Constitution. The Articles of Confederation mentioned treason as one of many crimes for which a person, once charged, could be extradited to the state in which the offense was committed.

> If any Person guilty of, or charged with, treason, felony, or other high misdemeanor in any state, shall flee from Justice, and be found in any of the united states, he shall upon demand of the Governor or executive power of the state from which he fled, be delivered up, and removed to the state having jurisdiction of his offence.
>
> —Article IV of the Articles of Confederation

From the perspective of the Articles, treason was a crime against a state government that was punishable by state law. By making treason a federal crime, the Constitution states that Americans owe loyalty not only to the government of the state in which they reside but also to the US government.

LEGAL DEFINITION OF TREASON

Article III, Section 3 of the Constitution gives a precise definition of treason: "Treason against the United States, shall consist only in levying War against them, or in adhering to their Enemies, giving them Aid and Comfort." Treason is the only federal crime specifically defined by the Constitution. While Congress can define the parameters of most crimes (like counterfeiting and tax evasion), anyone tried for treason under the Constitution must be found guilty of committing a specific act that falls under the definition of treason. The framers chose to include a specific definition for treason to prevent federal authorities from creating broad definitions to stifle political dissent.

Only a few years after the Constitution was ratified, Americans witnessed from afar the radical phase of the French Revolution when citizens were put to death for offenses as mundane as baking white bread or professing the Catholic religion. The First Amendment's guarantees of freedom of expression can be viewed as a companion to the Treason Clause, making it clear that expressing opposition to government policies is not a criminal offense.

Levying War

According to the Constitution, committing treason means that one must actually carry out an action that clearly makes war against the United States. In 1807, Aaron Burr was arrested for treason on the orders of President Thomas Jefferson. Burr had allegedly engaged in a conspiracy to embark on a military expedition to create an independent state on the frontier between the United States and Spanish Texas. Chief Justice John Marshall, who presided over Burr's trial in his capacity as a circuit-riding justice in Virginia, instructed the jury that a sentence of treason required evidence of action—a plan alone was not concrete proof. The jury acquitted Burr, who went into a self-imposed exile in Europe before returning to New York several years later.

Giving Aid and Comfort to the Enemy

Committing treason does not necessarily involve starting a war. A person can instead simply give aid and comfort to the enemy. As with making war, giving aid and comfort requires an action to be taken against the United States in cooperation with a foreign enemy. During the Cold War, Julius and Ethel Rosenberg were found guilty of espionage. They were convicted of spying for the Soviet Union and providing Soviet officials with important documents related to the Manhattan Project, which had produced the first atomic bomb. The Rosenbergs were executed in 1953 after a highly publicized trial. Technically, the Rosenbergs were not charged with treason, as the United States never declared war against the Soviet Union, but, in modern times, the charge of espionage has become synonymous with treason.

PUNISHMENT OF TREASON CLAUSE

In addition to clearly defining treason, the Constitution also sets limits on punishment for treason.

> The Congress shall have Power to declare the Punishment of Treason, but no Attainder of Treason shall work Corruption of Blood, or Forfeiture except during the Life of the Person attainted.
> —Article III, Section 3 of the Constitution

In the English legal tradition, a person who was attainted for treason not only forfeited their life and property; they also subjected their relatives and heirs to "corruption of blood." The children of an attainted individual could not inherit that person's estate. Although the government can seize the property of someone who commits treason, the property must be confiscated while the individual is still alive; otherwise, an individual's heirs maintain the right to inherit the property.

THE AMERICAN CIVIL WAR

Although Confederate leaders made war against the United States, no one was tried for treason in the Civil War's aftermath. Presidents Abraham Lincoln and Andrew Johnson sought to reconcile the nation, and they believed that treason trials would inhibit that process. Johnson made generous use of his pardoning power to grant amnesty to former Confederate leaders. Robert E. Lee, who led the Confederate Army of Northern Virginia in several battles against Union forces, assumed the presidency of Washington College, which is now Washington and Lee University. Confederate President Jefferson Davis was indicted for treason but was never tried.

In 1868, Johnson issued a blanket pardon for all former Confederate leaders, and the charges against Davis were dropped. In the 1970s, Presidents Ford and Carter signed joint congressional resolutions restoring the citizenship of Lee and Davis, respectively. However, recent reappraisals of the Civil War have prompted some to ask if clemency may have been awarded to Confederate leaders a bit too generously.

A CONCURRENT POWER?

Although the Constitution defines treason as a federal crime, states may have their own treason laws. The first person executed for treason under the Constitution was John Brown, who led a raid against a federal arsenal at Harpers Ferry, Virginia (now West Virginia). Although Brown's decision to target a federal facility was clear evidence of treason against the United States, the governor of Virginia arrived at Harpers Ferry ahead of federal authorities and demanded that Brown be prosecuted for treason against the Commonwealth of Virginia. Federal officials yielded to the governor's demand. Brown was tried in a Virginia court for the crime of "conspiring with negroes to produce insurrection," found guilty, and hanged by Virginia authorities. Though committing treason against a state might seem strange or unlikely today, Americans had strong allegiances to their states when the Constitution was written. Many states still have laws against treason.

A RARE CRIME

The Constitution's strict definition of treason has resulted in a very limited number of treason charges and trials in US history. As much attention as the trial of the Rosenbergs received in the 1950s in the early days of the Cold War, it did not lead to such trials becoming commonplace. The rarity of the charge of treason in the United States is a direct result of intentional efforts by the framers to reserve such a charge for the rarest of cases.

Chapter 6

The Law of the Land

Nearly 80 percent of the text of the original Constitution that was drafted by the framers at the Philadelphia Convention focuses on the structures and powers of the three branches of government. However, the structure and organization of the federal government do not account for the entire system of federalism established by the Constitution. Articles IV through VII of the Constitution provide answers regarding how the document will be ratified and amended, what the states can expect from each other and from the federal government, and the proper relationship between the federal government and state governments. The following sections provide more information about these issues.

FULL FAITH AND CREDIT

What the States Can Expect from Each Other

The Constitution was designed to bring the states together into "a more perfect Union" compared to the "firm league of friendship" established between them by the Articles of Confederation. However, a key part of constructing a more perfect union was to preserve the agreements reached between states in the Articles. The first two sections of Article IV of the Constitution are carried over from the Articles almost verbatim. Since the Constitution cements these previously established agreements, it is important to understand what the framers believed the Articles had gotten right.

FULL FAITH AND CREDIT CLAUSE

Both the Articles and the Constitution include a Full Faith and Credit Clause, which obligates every state to honor court judgments and contracts that carry legal weight in other states.

> Full Faith and Credit shall be given in each State to the public Acts, Records, and judicial Proceedings of every other State. And the Congress may by general Laws prescribe the Manner in which such Acts, Records and Proceedings shall be proved, and the Effect thereof.
>
> —Article IV, Section 1 of the Constitution

Because of the Full Faith and Credit Clause, a couple that gets married in one state does not have to get married again if they move to another state, and the ownership of the vehicles and property they bring with them are recognized in their new state of residence. If not for the Full Faith and Credit Clause, a person who gets a restraining order would lose the protections offered by that order as soon as they left the state where it was issued. Also, if a resident of one state drives through another state, their driver's license is valid in that state (although Americans are legally required to get a new driver's license after establishing residence in another state).

Although the Full Faith and Credit Clause guarantees that nearly all legal contracts and proceedings reached in one state are recognized in all of the others, there are some exceptions.

The Defense of Marriage Act

In 1996, Congress passed the Defense of Marriage Act (DOMA), which defined marriage as a contract between a man and a woman for purposes of federal law. Section 2 of DOMA exempted states from recognizing same-sex marriages contracted in other states. Critics of DOMA argued that Section 2 violated the Full Faith and Credit Clause by enabling states to refuse to recognize valid legal contracts from other states, while supporters of the law emphasized that the Full Faith and Credit Clause authorizes Congress to pass relevant legislation relating to contracts between the states. While there have been attempts to challenge Section 2 of DOMA in federal court on the basis of the Full Faith and Credit Clause, the Supreme Court never specifically ruled against the constitutionality of the provision (although it did rule against DOMA's definition of marriage as between a man and a woman in 2013).

The Supreme Court eventually ruled in *Obergefell v. Hodges* (2015) that same-sex marriages were constitutionally protected under the Fourteenth Amendment's Equal Protection Clause. When that happened, DOMA was effectively struck down in its entirety.

Concealed Carry Reciprocity

The Full Faith and Credit Clause does not obligate states to recognize concealed carry permits that are issued in other states, as these permits allow residents to carry concealed weapons in their home state. While there have been efforts in Congress to enact federal legislation that would require states to recognize out-of-state concealed carry permits, none of these efforts have resulted in the passage of a federal law. Although there is no federal law requiring states to recognize concealed carry permits from other states, many states have entered into reciprocity agreements with other states, with some states enacting full reciprocity and others being more selective about which states' permits they recognize.

PRIVILEGES AND IMMUNITIES CLAUSE

Article IV of the Constitution also contains the Privileges and Immunities Clause, which reads: "The Citizens of each State shall be entitled to all Privileges and Immunities of Citizens in the several States." The Privileges and Immunities Clause guarantees that a citizen of one state will not be treated like a second-class citizen in another state and that they will not be deprived of the privileges (benefits) and immunities (protections) that are available to the native-born citizens of that state.

Like the Full Faith and Credit Clause, the Privileges and Immunities Clause is carried over from the Articles of Confederation, which refers to "free inhabitants" rather than citizens, and explicitly excludes "paupers, vagabonds and fugitives from Justice" from the protections provided by the clause. Although the original Constitution does not specifically define citizenship, the Fourteenth Amendment confers citizenship on everyone born on American soil and restricts the states from abridging the privileges or immunities of citizens, effectively doubling down on the protections already offered in Article IV.

EXTRADITION CLAUSE

Article IV also includes the Extradition Clause, which is carried over from the Articles of Confederation.

> A Person charged in any State with Treason, Felony, or other Crime, who shall flee from Justice, and be found in another State, shall on Demand of the executive Authority of the State from which he fled, be delivered up, to be removed to the State having Jurisdiction of the Crime.
>
> —Article IV, Section 2, Clause 2 of the Constitution

The Extradition Clause ensures that a person who commits a crime in one state does not flee to another state in an effort to escape justice. This means that someone cannot steal a car in one state and escape justice by driving into another state. Police authorities in each state regularly cooperate with their counterparts in other states to ensure that criminals will be brought to justice.

FUGITIVE SLAVE CLAUSE

The Extradition Clause is followed by the closely related Fugitive Slave Clause, which obligated states to hand over any "Person held to Service or Labour in one State, under the Laws thereof, escaping into another." The Fugitive Slave Clause was rendered inoperable by the Thirteenth Amendment, which abolished slavery. The clause, which became a major point of contention between Northern and Southern states in the years preceding the Civil War, was made operable by two acts of Congress passed in 1793 and 1850.

Fugitive Slave Act of 1793

The framers were careful to never mention the word *slavery* in the Constitution, but the first federal law that enforced its provisions was titled somewhat bluntly. The Fugitive Slave Act of 1793 was the first act to legally sanction the pursuit of fugitives who escaped from slavery into the free states. It included a hefty fine for anyone caught harboring or aiding a fugitive enslaved person.

Fugitive Slave Act of 1850

Congress passed the Fugitive Slave Act of 1850 as part of a larger legislative package known as the Compromise of 1850 in response to refusals by authorities in Northern free states to apprehend and hand over people who had escaped from slavery. The federal law placed the enforcement of the law in federal hands and denied a jury trial to accused fugitives. Some Northern states resisted the law by passing personal liberty laws that guaranteed a jury trial to anyone in their state accused of being a fugitive slave.

NEW STATES AND FEDERAL TERRITORIES

Beyond the Original Thirteen States

The Constitution, as originally ratified, was an agreement between the original thirteen states (formerly known as the thirteen colonies). However, the Treaty of Paris (1783), which ended the Revolutionary War, granted the United States sovereignty over territory stretching to the Mississippi River. Over the course of the nineteenth century, Americans embraced the idea of "manifest destiny," believing that their country had been ordained to expand its borders across the continent. By 1898, the United States controlled an empire that exercised sovereignty from Puerto Rico to the Philippines. This territorial expansion was guided by Article IV, Section 3 of the Constitution, which provides for the admission of new states and the governance of federal territories.

ADMISSION OF NEW STATES

The Constitution authorizes Congress to admit new states into the union while requiring Congress to get the approval of any states whose borders would be altered by a new state's creation.

New States may be admitted by the Congress into this Union; but no new State shall be formed or erected within the Jurisdiction of any other State; nor any State be formed by the Junction of two or more States, or Parts of States, without the Consent of the Legislatures of the States concerned as well as of the Congress.

—Article IV, Section 3, Clause 1 of the Constitution

The Articles of Confederation had placed the admission of new states into the hands of the states, requiring the support of at least nine states. When the Articles were drafted, the United States did not have any federally administered territories, so it was presumed that any state joining the Confederation would be a newly independent colony that had broken away from Britain or another European power. When the British ceded lands west of the Appalachian Mountains as part of the peace settlement that ended the Revolutionary War, Congress organized the territory through the Northwest Ordinance of 1787. This ordinance organized the territory west of the Appalachian Mountains and north of the Ohio River (including the present-day states of Ohio and Michigan), creating a territorial government and setting the conditions for the creation of future states. Although the Articles of Confederation is known for its many inadequacies and failures, the Northwest Ordinance was not among them. The Constitution sought to pick up where the Northwest Ordinance left off.

When Congress creates a state from territory belonging to existing states, any states affected must give their permission. This happened for the first time in 1795, when Virginia allowed its trans-Appalachian territory to join the Union as the state of Kentucky. In 1820, Massachusetts allowed its noncontiguous Maine District to form a separate state, giving New England the added benefit of two additional senators at a time when the region's influence was declining due to westward expansion. Following Virginia's secession ordinance in 1861, Unionists in the western region of Virginia organized themselves into the Restored Government of Virginia. Congress then recognized the Restored Government of Virginia as the legitimate state government of Virginia, allowing this provisional legislature to authorize the creation of the state of West Virginia in 1863.

Although new states do not get a stripe on the flag, they do get a star as well as every privilege that comes with statehood. The admission of thirty-seven new states to the Union since the ratification of the Constitution is a visible expression of Thomas Jefferson's dream of an Empire of Liberty, in which the United States plays a major role in spreading the values of freedom and democratic republicanism throughout the Americas and across the globe.

ADMINISTERING FEDERAL TERRITORIES

The Property Clause of the Constitution authorizes Congress to organize governments in federal territories and properties.

> The Congress shall have Power to dispose of and make all needful Rules and Regulations respecting the Territory or other Property belonging to the United States.
>
> —Article IV, Section 3, Clause 2 of the Constitution

Federal territories consist of all land claimed by the US government that is not a part of any state. For much of early US history, territory was acquired with the intent of creating new states. By 1853, the present-day boundaries of the contiguous United States on the North American continent had been established. All of this territory is now claimed by the contiguous forty-eight states. Beginning with the Alaska Purchase in 1867, the United States added territories outside of its contiguous domain with no intention of creating states out of these territories. (Alaska became a state in 1959, over ninety years after the US purchased the land.)

The Spanish-American War

In 1898, the United States declared war against Spain, beginning a short-lived war that resulted in the purchase of Puerto Rico, Guam, and the Philippines from Spain. Unlike previous territorial acquisitions, the US had no intention of admitting any of these territories as states. American military forces were sent to the Philippines to crush an independence movement, which led to the formation of the American Anti-Imperialist League. The members of this organization believed that the forced subjugation of Filipinos was a betrayal of American values.

The Annexation of Hawaii

In the same year as the Spanish-American War, the United States annexed Hawaii. The island's sugar crops and strategic location in the middle of the Pacific Ocean offered to boost American fortunes and military clout.

The Insular Cases

A series of Supreme Court decisions in the early twentieth century led to the doctrine stating that the inhabitants of federal overseas territories are not automatically entitled to constitutional rights unless congressional legislation conferred these rights upon them. However, Congress granted citizenship to Hawaiians in 1900 and Puerto Ricans in 1917. Filipinos were never granted citizenship; instead, the United States granted independence to the Philippines in 1946. Today, while most inhabitants of American territories have the benefits of US citizenship, residents of American Samoa lack the benefits of birthright citizenship and are legally considered US nationals rather than citizens.

The Question of Puerto Rican Statehood

In recent years, Puerto Rico has held several referendums on statehood. These have shown mixed results, reflecting the complex views of Puerto Ricans on this issue. Proponents of statehood argue that it would provide equal rights and representation, while opponents express concerns about preserving cultural identity and autonomy. As of today, Puerto Rico remains a territory, and the decision about its future status is complex, involving both the will of its people and the approval of the US Congress. This situation exemplifies the broader challenges and considerations in changing the status of a US territory.

TERRITORIES AND AMERICAN IDENTITY

Today, the United States' overseas territories offer a unique perspective on American governance and identity. Many now question what American identity is, and whether the US will welcome an additional state. According to the US Census Bureau, in 2020, nearly 20 percent of Americans identified as Hispanic, so Spanish-speaking Puerto Rico becoming a state may not seem as far-fetched as it did a century ago.

CONSTITUTIONAL GUARANTEES TO THE STATES

What the States Can Expect from the Federal Government

Article IV of the Constitution includes three guarantees that the federal government makes to every state. In a federal republic, it is important that a republican form of government be maintained at both the federal and the state levels. The states are also entitled to security under the Constitution from both invasions and insurrectionary violence. These guarantees are summed up in the Constitution's Guarantee Clause.

> The United States shall guarantee to every State in this Union a Republican Form of Government, and shall protect each of them against Invasion; and on Application of the Legislature, or of the Executive (when the Legislature cannot be convened) against domestic Violence.
>
> —Article IV, Section 4 of the Constitution

A REPUBLICAN FORM OF GOVERNMENT

The Constitution guarantees that every state will have a republican form of government. A republic is generally understood to be a government without a king, in which the people exercise their sovereign authority through elected representatives. In Federalist No. 39, James Madison defines a republican form of government as "a government which derives all its powers directly or indirectly from the great body of the people, and is administered by persons holding their offices during pleasure, for a limited period, or during good behavior."

In the two centuries since the ratification of the Constitution, American understanding of republicanism has evolved, and the Constitution's guarantee of a republican form of government for every state offers the states both flexibility and restrictions in the organizing of their republican governments.

Structuring State Governments

Each state is permitted to structure its own government within the bounds of republicanism. Although every state's executive branch is administered by a popularly elected governor, states aren't prohibited from having an executive committee run the legislative branch or from having a governor who is appointed by the legislature.

States also have some flexibility in structuring their legislative branches. Although forty-nine states have bicameral legislatures, Nebraska has a unicameral legislature, which was established in the 1930s as a measure to make the state government less expensive and more efficient during the Great Depression. As with other states, Nebraskans get to vote for their elected representatives, so their legislature meets the basic criteria for a republican form of government. This unique legislative arrangement shows how states can experiment with different structures in the federal democratic republic established by the Constitution.

Term Limits

Each state can decide for itself whether and how to limit the terms of elected officials. Depending on the state, a governor may have a two-year or a four-year term in office. Governors of some states are limited to one term, others to one consecutive term, others to two terms, and still others are not term-limited at all. In the 1990s, several states passed legislative term limits, restricting the terms of state legislators to anywhere between eight and twelve years.

The Reconstruction Acts

In 1867, two years after the conclusion of the Civil War, congressional Republicans passed the first of four Reconstruction Acts. These acts disestablished the existing state governments of ten of the eleven former Confederate states (except Tennessee) and organized them into five military districts. Congress justified the act by claiming that the governments in these states did not meet the requirements for a republican form of government under the Guarantee Clause.

The following year, Georgia, Florida, and Alabama, which had been placed in the Third Military District, sued Secretary of War Edwin Stanton, claiming that the disestablishment of their state governments violated the Constitution. The Supreme Court declined to rule on the case, as the justices saw this as a "political question" that did not involve specific persons or property. So, the military governments established in the former Confederacy remained in place until the state governments were reestablished by actions taken by the legislative and executive branches. Congress has never again invoked the Guarantee Clause against a state's government.

The Fourteenth Amendment

By defining citizenship by birth and granting every citizen the equal protection of the laws, the Fourteenth Amendment represents an evolving understanding of democratic republicanism. While the framers didn't consider universal suffrage to be a necessary component of republicanism (and found the idea of democracy to be frightening and dangerous), contemporary Americans view democratic ideals of political equality—without regard to race, gender, or property ownership—as foundational to their understanding of republicanism.

Baker v. Carr

During the civil rights movement, the Supreme Court began to participate in political questions, deciding in *Baker v. Carr* (1962) that federal courts could intervene to restrict states from drawing electoral districts of unequal size. The *Baker* decision established the principle of "one person, one vote," mandating that the states draw legislative districts (for both Congress and state legislatures) that are roughly equal in population.

Voting Rights Act of 1965

In 1965, Congress passed the Voting Rights Act, authorizing the federal government to supervise elections in states and counties (particularly in the South) that had documented histories of voter suppression, intimidation, and discrimination. The Voting Rights Act required states with histories of discrimination to receive clearance from the Justice Department before changing election laws or redrawing congressional districts.

Shaw v. Reno

One court case that resulted from the Voting Rights Act was *Shaw v. Reno* (1993), in which a North Carolina resident challenged a Justice Department's mandate. This mandate stated that North Carolina must create an additional "majority-minority" district so that the state's Black voters could receive additional representation in Congress. The Supreme Court struck down the specific district, as there was no explanation for the district's existence other than race. However, the Court upheld the constitutionality of majority-minority districts as long as race was not the sole factor in their creation.

PROTECTION FROM INVASION

The Constitution guarantees that the federal government will protect the states from invasion; however, the Constitution doesn't define "invasion." In the context of international law, an invasion is understood to be an act of aggression by one nation against another, including a large and organized body of armed troops. However, an invasion can also be loosely understood to describe any unwanted arrival of a large group of people.

An Invasion of Texas?

In 2024, Texas Governor Greg Abbott invoked a loose definition of invasion in an executive order calling for the Texas National Guard and state law enforcement agencies to patrol the international border between Texas and Mexico. There had been an unprecedented number of unauthorized border crossings during the previous year, and Abbott argued that the federal government was not doing its duty of protecting the states from invasion.

PROTECTION AGAINST DOMESTIC VIOLENCE

The phrase *domestic violence* is typically used today in reference to physical altercations among members of a single household, but the framers used it to refer to rebellions and insurrections within a state (as opposed to a foreign invasion). One of the major catalysts for the Constitutional Convention was Shays' Rebellion, which nearly overthrew the elected state government of Massachusetts. The Constitution authorizes state governments to request federal assistance when insurrectionary activity exceeds a state's capacity to contain it, accomplishing the Preamble's aspirations of domestic tranquility.

THE SUPREMACY CLAUSE

Establishing the Supreme Law of the Land

Article VI declares that the Constitution is the supreme law of the land, making all federal and state laws subordinate to it. As it is only followed by Article VII, which briefly describes the ratification process, Article VI functions as the original Constitution's last words, tying up a few loose ends not addressed previously. Its three brief clauses validate debts that were incurred by the United States under the Articles of Confederation, proclaim the Constitution as the supreme law of the land, and obligate both federal and state officials to swear oaths supporting the Constitution.

VALIDATING THE PUBLIC DEBT

All Debts contracted and Engagements entered into, before the Adoption of this Constitution, shall be as valid against the United States under this Constitution, as under the Confederation.

—Article VI, Clause 1 of the Constitution

Because the Constitutional Convention was called partly to address the debt crisis that followed the Revolutionary War, the framers wanted to clarify that the Constitution was not an attempt to avoid paying the government's debts. The Constitution's government would be prepared to use its powers over taxation and commerce to begin paying its debts and building public credit. Alexander Hamilton, the first secretary of the treasury, really had his work cut out for him. His proposal to pay all US debts at face value (rather than at twenty-five cents on the dollar) aligned with the Constitution's aspirations to create a sound financial system, in which all contracted debts would be paid in full.

THE SUPREMACY CLAUSE

The focal point of Article VI is the Supremacy Clause, which declares the Constitution, along with all federal laws and treaties enacted in accordance with it, to be absolute.

> This Constitution, and the Laws of the United States which shall be made in Pursuance thereof; and all Treaties made, or which shall be made, under the Authority of the United States, shall be the supreme Law of the Land; and the Judges in every State shall be bound thereby.
>
> —Article VI, Clause 2 of the Constitution

The Supremacy Clause mandates that state governments not only follow their own laws but also abide by treaties, laws passed by Congress, and judgments of the Supreme Court. Judges in state courts cannot hand down judgments that would give precedence to state laws over federal laws. If a state law conflicts with a constitutional federal law, it is invalid.

Ratification Debates

The Supremacy Clause was a target of Antifederalist writers who employed an overly simplistic reading of the clause that presumed that it would result in federal laws being superior to state laws in all cases. Prominent Antifederalist Brutus argued that the Supremacy

Clause would effectively shut down the state governments, making "laws of every state...nullified and declared void."

In Federalist No. 33, Alexander Hamilton responded to Brutus and other Antifederalists that the Supremacy Clause was necessary and harmless to the states. The clause simply clarified that federal laws would supersede state laws *when Congress acts in accordance with the Constitution*. Hamilton argued that there was no threat to the reserved powers of the states since the clause did not authorize Congress to legislate beyond the limits of its delegated powers. Additionally, if Congress were to pass an unconstitutional law, the Supremacy Clause would do nothing to give that law any validity.

"In Pursuance Thereof"

The Supremacy Clause is commonly misinterpreted as granting Congress carte blanche to pass any law it wants. Those who subscribe to this misinterpretation forget to read the phrase "in pursuance thereof," which clearly indicates that in order for a federal law to become part of the supreme law of the land, it has to be made in pursuit of a clear constitutional objective.

Hamilton's analysis of the Supremacy Clause has been supported by the Supreme Court, which has upheld and struck down federal laws through its power of judicial review. In *McCulloch v. Maryland* (1819), the Court ruled in favor of the Bank of the United States against the state of Maryland. Maryland had unsuccessfully tried to tax the federally chartered institution. John Marshall sided with the bank not because it had been established by federal law but because he believed that the federal law that established it had a clear constitutional basis in the financial powers delegated to Congress in

Article I, Section 8. The other side of the coin is the Supreme Court's decision in *United States v. Lopez* (1995), which struck down the Gun-Free School Zones Act of 1990 because Congress had exceeded its authority under the Commerce Clause. The *Lopez* decision demonstrates that the Supremacy Clause does not subordinate the states to the federal government in all cases. Congressional legislation takes precedence over state laws only when the legislation is grounded in a delegated power.

OATHS OF OFFICE

Although the president's oath of office is specifically prescribed in Article II, the first three Articles of the Constitution do not prescribe any oaths for other government officials. Article VI, Clause 2 mandates that both federal and state government officials must take an oath to support the Constitution. The requirement that both state and federal officials swear oaths demonstrates that all government officials have a duty to support the Constitution.

NO RELIGIOUS TEST

The Constitution clearly states that "no religious Test shall ever be required as a Qualification to any Office or public Trust under the United States." The prohibition of religious tests demonstrates the influence of Enlightenment ideals of secularism and religious toleration on the creation of the Constitution.

AMENDING THE CONSTITUTION

Forming an Even More Perfect Union

The greatest flaw of the Articles of Confederation was the near impossibility of amending them. Amending the Articles would have required the consent of *every single state*. Consider how difficult it would be today to get thirteen separate political communities to agree on the same change to a governing document. To amend a constitution, the states must not only agree on the problem; they must also picture the same type of solution. Such a degree of unanimity is technically possible, but it is highly improbable. It is no wonder the Articles were never amended. Article V of the Constitution sets the procedures by which constitutional amendments can be proposed and ratified.

PROPOSING AMENDMENTS

The first step in amending the Constitution is proposing an amendment. Of course, proposed amendments can either be ratified or rejected. The Constitution offers two processes by which amendments can be proposed.

> The Congress, whenever two thirds of both Houses shall deem it necessary, shall propose Amendments to this Constitution, or, on the Application of the Legislatures of two thirds of the several States, shall call a Convention for proposing Amendments.
>
> —Article V of the Constitution

The first method for proposing amendments is for an amendment to gain the approval of two-thirds of both houses of Congress. This is certainly no small task, as it requires a consensus in both houses, which cannot be accomplished without support from many different kinds of states. This method has been used to propose all thirty-three amendments that have been proposed since the Constitution's existence.

The Constitution provides a second way to propose amendments by allowing two-thirds of the state legislatures to petition Congress to call a convention of states to propose amendments. As of this book's release, an Article V Convention has never been called under the existence of the Constitution.

Although an Article V Convention has never been called, it is not outside the realm of possibility that such a convention may be called in the future. Many Americans support congressional term limits and balanced budgets during peacetime, but Congress is not likely to ever propose an amendment that will restrict its powers. As of 2024, nineteen states (out of the required thirty-four) have passed resolutions calling for an Article V Convention to propose amendments for congressional term limits, a limit on borrowing, and a more precise definition of the Commerce Clause. When describing the amendment process in Federalist No. 43, James Madison argued that the ability of both Congress and the states to initiate the amendment process was a strength that indicated the Constitution's flexibility. Although an Article V Convention is an interesting idea, Congress has been the exclusive initiator of constitutional amendments in the years since the Constitution was ratified.

THREE-FOURTHS OF THE STATES

Regardless of the method of initiation, every amendment to the Constitution must be ratified by three-fourths of the states to take effect. While getting three-fourths of the states to agree on a constitutional amendment is not an easy task, it is far from impossible. Madison defended the three-fourths threshold in Federalist No. 43, explaining that the amendment process "guards equally against that extreme facility which would render the Constitution too mutable; and that extreme difficulty which might perpetuate its discovered faults." As a plan of government, the Constitution should have some flexibility when obvious faults are discovered (such as the initial method of electing the president and vice president on one ballot). That said, it should also have a high degree of stability, offering Americans reasonable assurance concerning the continuity and strength of their government.

ERAS OF AMENDMENT

One could compare constitutional amendments to wolves, as they both seem to prefer to travel in packs. While a "lone wolf" amendment may show up once in a while, most of the twenty-seven amendments to the Constitution have been ratified in proximity to similar amendments. Here are some of the popular eras.

- The first ten amendments that make up the Bill of Rights were added to the Constitution shortly after ratification. These amendments were all designed to protect the rights of the people and the states from encroachments by the federal government.
- The Reconstruction Amendments (Thirteenth through Fifteenth) were ratified in the years immediately following the Civil War. These amendments abolished slavery, guaranteed birthright citizenship with equal protection of the laws, and prohibited voter discrimination on the basis of race, color, or previous condition of servitude.

- The Progressive Amendments (Sixteenth through Nineteenth) were ratified during the second decade of the twentieth century amid reforms that increased the scope of the federal government and expanded democracy. These amendments included the federal income tax, direct election of senators, prohibition of alcohol, and women's suffrage.

FAILED AMENDMENTS

Given that it takes a high level of consensus to pass a proposed amendment through both houses of Congress, it is no wonder that twenty-seven of the thirty-three amendments that Congress has proposed have been ratified by the states. However, there were some notable attempts at amending the Constitution that were never ratified.

- In 1810, an amendment to prohibit Americans from accepting titles of nobility from foreign governments (the consequence being loss of citizenship) passed overwhelmingly in both the Senate and the House, but it fell one state short in its quest for ratification.
- In 1861, in response to the secession crisis and the formation of the Confederacy, Congress passed the Corwin Amendment, which would have made it impossible to amend the Constitution in a way that would prohibit slavery in any state. This amendment lost steam when it failed to end the secession crisis.
- In 1972, Congress passed the Equal Rights Amendment (ERA), which would have constitutionally prohibited discrimination "on account of sex." The ERA was on its way to ratification when conservative women, worried about unintended consequences, launched the

"STOP ERA" campaign, killing support in wavering states. That said, the Civil Rights Act of 1964 prohibits discrimination based on sex, gender identity, and sexual orientation.

WILL THERE BE MORE AMENDMENTS?

The Constitution has not been formally amended since 1992 when a college student launched a campaign to ratify one of James Madison's originally proposed amendments regarding congressional pay raises. However, this amendment was proposed by Congress two centuries before it was ratified. The ratification of the Twenty-Sixth Amendment in 1971 was the last time an amendment was proposed by Congress and ratified by the states within a short period of time. Congress hasn't proposed a single amendment to the states since 1978, when a proposed amendment to give Washington, DC, representation in Congress received a cold reception (only sixteen states voted to ratify it). Perhaps, asking two-thirds of both houses of Congress and three-fourths of the states to agree to an amendment today is not so different from the unanimity threshold set by the Articles of Confederation.

Regardless of whether the Constitution is amended again in this century, it has served Americans quite well for over two centuries with minimal amendment. And though it has a complex history, this plan of government conceived in Philadelphia over 230 years ago (with a few improvements added since) still provides a framework today for the largest presidential republic on earth to be governed by "We the People."

INDEX